Internal Accounting Systems and Controls

Tutorial

Sheriden Amos
Michael Fardon

© Sheriden Amos, Michael Fardon, 2022.

All rights reserved. No part of this publication may be reproduced, stored in a retrieval system, or transmitted in any form or by any means, electronic, mechanical, photo-copying, recording or otherwise, without the prior consent of the copyright owners, or in accordance with the provisions of the Copyright, Designs and Patents Act 1988, or under the terms of any licence permitting limited copying issued by the Copyright Licensing Agency, Saffron House, 6-10 Kirby Street, London EC1N 8TS.

Published by Osborne Books Limited
Tel 01905 748071
Email books@osbornebooks.co.uk
Website www.osbornebooks.co.uk

Design by Laura Ingham

Printed by CPI Group (UK) Limited, Croydon, CR0 4YY, on environmentally friendly, acid-free paper from managed forests.

British Library Cataloguing in Publication Data
A catalogue record for this book is available from the British Library

ISBN 978-1-911198-72-7

Contents

Introduction

Qualifications covered

This book has been written specifically to cover the Unit 'Internal Accounting Systems and Controls' which is mandatory for the following qualifications:

AAT Level 4 Diploma in Professional Accounting

AAT Diploma in Professional Accounting – SCQF Level 8

The book contains a clear text with worked examples and case studies, chapter summaries and key terms to help with revision. Each chapter concludes with a wide range of activities, many in the style of AAT computer based assessments.

Pre-released scenario and reference material is available to you ahead of the assessment. Studying this will encourage you to think about the areas the assessment covers.

Osborne Study and Revision Materials

Additional materials, tailored to the needs of students studying this Unit and revising for the assessment, include:

- **Workbooks:** paperback books with practice activities and exams
- **Student Zone:** access to Osborne Books online resources
- **Osborne Books App:** Osborne Books ebooks for mobiles and tablets

Visit www.osbornebooks.co.uk for details of study and revision resources and access to online material.

1 Introduction to internal accounting systems and controls

this chapter covers...

This first chapter is an introduction to the Unit 'Internal Accounting Systems and Controls.' The chapter will explain:

■ *the subject areas covered by this assessment*

■ *the focus of the different tasks in the assessment*

The chapter concludes with a Case Study which gives an idea of what to expect in the AAT scenario and reference materials for this assessment.

INTRODUCTION TO THE UNIT

what this Unit involves

The Unit 'Internal Accounting Systems and Controls' combines five AAT Learning Outcomes which will be assessed in the assessment:

■ understand the role and responsibilities of the accounting function within an organisation

■ evaluate internal control systems

■ evaluate an organisation's accounting system and underpinning procedures

■ understand the impact of technology on accounting systems

■ recommend improvements to an organisation's accounting system

what you will learn

When you have completed this Unit you should be able to:

■ **understand the role of accounting** in an organisation in supporting different departments of the organisation and dealing with outside organisations and individuals

■ understand the importance and principles of **internal control** of the accounting function in an organisation – to help efficiency and to identify potential fraud and breaches of professional ethics

■ **evaluate accounting systems**

– identify the requirements of accounting systems

– work out the improvements that could be made to limit the risk of fraud occurring

– make suggestions as to how the improvements could be implemented

– identify the impact that the changes would make on the system and its users, suggesting methods to support users during such changes

■ **consider how technology** can affect the accounting system, both in terms of the benefits of using technology, such as cloud accounting, and risks it poses to the business

■ **review a planned system change** and make suitable recommendations to ensure that the integrity of the accounting system is maintained

WHAT YOU WILL NEED TO KNOW – AN OVERVIEW

You will find this Unit will give you the opportunity to view a business from the perspective of a consultant. The foundations for this Unit are taught in the Level 3 Business Awareness Unit, and this Unit builds on this knowledge, some of which we will recap in the following chapters.

For this Unit, the assessment will include tasks where you:

- **consider the purpose, structure and organisation of the accounting function** and how these affect the accounting function and the technology used by it to make systems accurate, efficient and cost effective

- **consider fraud** and how to prevent and detect it

- **consider whether internal controls are effective**, deciding whether they are suitable and promote ethical and sustainable practices

- **review a current accounting system**, focusing on record keeping systems, principles of internal control, methods of fraud prevention and issues relating to professional ethics and sustainability

- **analyse a current accounting system**, identifying weaknesses or areas where improvement could be made and making recommendations to improve the system, bearing in mind all the costs involved

The assessment will be based on a scenario and reference materials, produced by the AAT, which is available to you to review prior to the assessment date. This will help you familiarise yourself with the business, prior to reviewing.

This overview is intended to give you an idea of what you need to know for this assessment. The chapters that follow broadly cover the material in this order. You should note that not every area will be covered in an individual assessment. However, over time, all areas will be tested so you need to ensure you are confident in every area prior to taking the assessment.

initial review of an organisation, using the scenario and reference materials

Review the scenario and reference materials to:

- define the structure, purpose and organisation of the **accounting function** within the overall organisation

- identify the **relationship** between the accounting function and the other internal departments

- identify the important **external relationship**s the organisation is likely to maintain; this could include relationships with customers, suppliers, shareholders, banks, trade organisations and governmental bodies such as HM Revenue & Customs

- decide **what an organisation requires from its accounting systems** – these requirements will differ depending on the nature and size of the organisation and will often use technology

review of an accounting system and internal controls

You will need to **review parts of an accounting system and the internal controls within it** to ensure that they meet the requirements of the organisation. In short . . .

- how good is the system?

- do things go wrong?

- could things go wrong?

This review could involve:

- evaluating an accounting system including, for example, sales, purchases, payments and receipts, payroll, petty cash, capital expenditure, inventory and expenses

- identifying the **strengths and weaknesses** of parts of an accounting system – this could include a review of the working methods used within an accounting system to ensure that the best results are being achieved especially in terms of cost-effectiveness, reliability and speed

- identifying the **external regulations** that will influence the way an accounting system will operate (eg legislation affecting payroll, or VAT regulations)

- **reviewing and evaluating the internal controls within the system** by identifying areas where there is a **potential for error**

- **reviewing and evaluating the internal control system** by identifying areas where there is a **potential for fraud** involving loss of money, inventory or working time, and then assessing the level of risk of that fraud – ie how likely it is

- identifying **ways of detecting fraud** and the types of **internal controls** that could be established to **prevent fraud** occurring

- identifying breaches or threats to the fundamental principles of **professional ethics**, eg petty theft in the workplace

- assessing the extent to which the accounting system fulfils the requirements of **sustainability** principles (eg by recycling resources, saving energy and by encouraging cycling to work)

- **reviewing weaknesses** that have been identified in the accounting system and explaining their impact upon the organisation – in terms of time, money and reputation (for example the loss of revenue, wasting time, letting customers down)

- **reviewing the use of technology** in the accounting system, such as cloud accounting, artificial intelligence, machine learning and data analytics, and explaining its impact upon the organisation

- **reviewing data security and the measures in place to protect data and operations** so the business can continue to operate successfully

- reviewing where there is a **change in accounting system** to determine the controls needed to move from the old to new system

making recommendations

You may need to be able to make clear and sensible recommendations to rectify weaknesses identified in your evaluation of the accounting systems:

- where you identify a weakness you need to offer a **recommendation** to rectify it

- you may be asked to work out the **cost of the recommendations** you are making, for example the cost of training, new computers, and the **benefits they will provide**; the need for staff training is very important

- you may be asked to **justify the changes** you want to make to management

HOW TO TACKLE THE ASSESSMENT

The processes described so far may sound complicated, but when you have finished this chapter you should be much more familiar with what is required and see how it all fits together, to help you pass the assessment.

There are two processes involved:

1	Learn the theory

2	Apply the theory

1

learn the theory

In order to be able to assess an organisation and its accounting system, you will need to acquire basic knowledge about areas such as:

- types of organisation – their needs and links with the commercial world

- accounting systems – their areas of activity and how they link with the rest of the organisation

- internal control systems

- the dangers of fraud and the levels of risk involved

- effective accounting systems and how they produce reliable and accurate information

- the impact of technology on the accounting system

- the ethical code, set out by the AAT

- the need for sustainability and practical ways of achieving it

- cost-benefit analysis – how to assess the benefits of a recommendation in relation to its costs

All these theoretical areas are covered in the chapters that immediately follow this one. These are:

Chapter 2 **The accounting function – how it works**

This explains the way in which accounting systems work, how they support the organisation and how they relate to outside bodies.

Chapter 3 **Stakeholders and their information needs**

This explains the various stakeholders in an organisation and how the management information systems are designed to provide them all with the information they need, including performance indicators, such as ratios.

Chapter 4 **Internal control systems and fraud**

This explains the way in which an organisation and its accounting system could exercise control over its operations.

This also explains the types of fraud and how fraud can affect organisations, as well as how to prevent and detect it.

Chapter 5   **Technology and accounting systems**

This explains the impact of technology on accounting systems and the types of new technologies available, such as artificial intelligence and data analytics, as well as how financial information can be presented to employees and clients.

This also explains the types of risks to data and operations.

Chapter 6   **Effective accounting systems**

This explains the different types of systems needed in an organisation and how they promote ethical and sustainable practices.

2   **apply the theory – review the system and make recommendations**

When you are confident of your knowledge in these areas, you will be able to:

■ **review** an accounting system

■ make **recommendations** for improvement

■ assess the **benefits** of a recommendation in relation to its costs

This is covered in:

Chapter 7   **Evaluation and review of an accounting system**

This will explain how you can review and evaluate an accounting system and determine weaknesses within it.

Chapter 8   **Recommendations and making changes**

This will explain the reasons for making changes to procedures and systems and the benefits of making them, along with any possible problems that may need resolving when changes are made.

Tackling the Assessment

Learning from this book:

- about the accounting systems within organisations
- study internal control and fraud and how to evaluate the effectiveness of a system
- study technology and its impact on accounting systems
- consider how ethics and sustainability influence the accounting systems
- what recommendations could be made to improve the systems

Apply the theory:

- complete the chapter activities
- practise using the AAT Sample Assessments

Study the scenario and reference material for your assessment

- consider the areas in the business which could be the focus for the assessment

Sit the assessment!

THE ASSESSMENT – SETTING THE SCENE

The assessment questions will be set around a business and to help you think about the issues it might face, the AAT has decided to give students access to some material prior to the day you sit the assessment at the computer. This 'scenario and reference material' explains:

- the **industry** the business is involved in and how long the business has been trading for – is it new or established?

- the **structure** of the business and the way in which it operates – for example, how does it sell its products?

- the **key personnel** in the business, including in the accounts department – how large is it?

- recent **developments** in the company – is it growing, in a competitive market or facing increasing regulation?

- **sustainability** issues – what economic, social and environmental issues does it face?

The following Case Study follows the pattern of the AAT material currently available, to give you an idea of what you can analyse prior to the exam. We will use this business as we go through the book to illustrate the different aspects of the unit.

Case Study

DESIGN FOR LIFE LTD

Design For Life Ltd (DFL) is a manufacturing business, producing well designed, sustainably produced and high quality furniture. It sells to end customers via two showrooms in Manchester and Birmingham in the UK and through independent retailers both in the UK and abroad. It has a factory in Birmingham and has online sales, via a website, which has recently led to increased sales.

Following this period of recent expansion, Design For Life Ltd has asked you, Sasha Mutahi, an Accounting Technician, to review the processes of the company. You are to identify weaknesses in the internal controls that may have occurred due to the recent growth of the company.

Company background

history

It was established seven years ago by Conrad Rumney and Edyta Whyte, who jointly own and run the business. They had both worked together in a similar business for many years, before deciding to design and produce their own furniture.

The company operates a manufacturing division and a sales division. The manufacturing division supplies furniture to the sales division, which sells both its own manufactured products and other ranges of furniture that complement its own, which it buys in from third parties, some of which are imported.

DFL's head office is in Birmingham, where its management team and finance department are both based. Its main manufacturing plant is also on this site, as are the sales division's offices and large central warehouse.

recent developments

Intense competition from overseas manufacturers, made worse by the strength of the pound, has led to a downwards pressure on market prices within the areas in which DFL traditionally operates in the last two years. DFL has been working on more affordable and sustainable designs, using materials such as bamboo, to increase sales.

It has also recently started offering a bespoke furniture service, due to growing demand in this area. Currently, this service is based in a small factory in Birmingham, near the main production site.

Sustainability

DFL relies on a highly skilled workforce, so its staff are an important resource. 'Craftsmanship' is more than simply 'training', so apprenticeships are offered to new employees, who often stay for many years. It also considers 'up skilling' where possible to ensure continued availability of skilled labour and a strong design team.

Reduction of waste in production is also important and it uses new materials and technologies, where possible, to achieve this.

The business is aiming to be carbon neutral by 2030. It has purchased several electric delivery vehicles and recycles wooden and cardboard packaging. It has implemented energy saving initiatives in all its buildings, including ground source heat pumps for heating and solar panels, with batteries, for lighting and hot water.

Suppliers are thoroughly vetted to ensure materials are sustainably produced, staff are paid fair wages and the working conditions are good.

Staff

DFL's key personnel are as follows:

Managing Director	Conrad Rumney
Operations Director	Juliette Swanson
Finance Director	Joseph Armstrong
Production Director	David Duke
Sales Director	Edyta White
Financial Controller	Aneysha Dickson
Purchasing Manager	Matt Arnold
Warehouse Manager	Andrew Roberts
Credit Controller	Salam Khan
Accounts Payable Clerk	Tina Fay
Accounts Receivable Clerk	Lila Firkin
General Accounts Clerk and Cashier	Ricardo Cox
Payroll Clerk	Petra Stanya

2 The accounting function – how it works

this chapter covers...

In this chapter we examine the way in which the accounting function 'fits into' the overall structure of the organisation and how it relates to other organisations.

The areas the chapter covers include:

- *how what an organisation does – ie its 'business' – affects its accounting function*
- *the overall structure of the organisation*
- *the structure of the accounting system*
- *how the accounting system interacts with the other functions*
- *the administrative systems and control of resources within the organisation*
- *the uses of the financial statements of the organisation*
- *the impact on an accounting system of regulations and legislation*

THE 'BUSINESS' OF THE ORGANISATION

public and private sectors

Organisations are normally classed as public sector or private sector.

Public sector organisations are those owned or controlled directly or indirectly by the state. They include corporations like the BBC, Government Departments and local authorities. Their function is largely to provide some form of service: broadcasting, health, education, policing, refuse collection, tax collection, for example. Some public sector organisations form partnerships with private sector companies to provide a service, eg hospitals in the National Health Service.

Private sector organisations, on the other hand, are in private ownership, and include businesses ranging from the sole trader to the public limited company. The function of these organisations is to provide a product such as a car or TV, or a service such as a holiday or a foot massage.

The range of activities carried out by both public and private sector organisations – the nature of their 'business' – can therefore be classified as:

- providing goods – either through manufacturing or through retailing

- providing a service – either for consumers (private sector) or as a social benefit (public sector)

You may not consider that tax collection is a social benefit, but if you appreciate that tax revenue is used for Government spending on health and education, you will see the logic.

how the 'business' affects the accounting system

All organisations need accounting systems to carry out the accounting function. This function includes:

- processing and recording financial transactions – keeping accounts
- payroll
- costing and budgeting
- raising finance

You will see from this list that these are 'generic' functions which are common to all organisations. The variation is in the detail and will depend on the type of 'business' the organisation carries out:

- a manufacturing company in the private sector, for example, will keep accounts for suppliers and customers, will run payroll and will cost and budget for the manufacturing process and other activities; it is likely to raise finance from banks and possibly the equity markets

■ a local authority in the public sector will keep accounts for suppliers and to a lesser extent for customers (council tax payers); it will run payroll and keep to strict budgets; its financing, however, will come from Central Government, local enterprises and from local taxation

We will look at effective accounting systems in Chapter 6 and consider how to evaluate an accounting system in Chapter 7.

ORGANISATIONAL STRUCTURE

The organisation of the accounting system will depend a great deal on the way in which the organisation as a whole is structured.

In the case of a smaller organisation such as a private company, the structure will be based on the shareholder directors being in charge of the whole business, with possibly a Finance Director in charge of the finance and accounting function. The variation arises when the organisation is larger, in which case the structure is likely to be either:

■ a loosely organised group of independent operating units, directed by a managing company, or

■ driven from the top and tightly controlled as a single unit

These are represented by the two basic types of organisational structure: decentralised and centralised.

decentralised structure – large organisation

This is where operating divisions of an organisation are relatively independent, and are likely to have their own accounting systems; the structure is 'flat'. A typical example is where groups of companies are divided up in terms of geographical areas or products. It must be stressed that it will be the responsibility of the managing company to ensure that the accounting systems of the separate companies are harmonised and work together. Study the diagram at the top of the next page.

Each manager is likely to be directly responsible for many staff, having a large span of control. This results in fewer levels of employee, from the directors down to the person at the lowest level, known as the length of the scalar chain – it will be short in this type of organisation. Information can be communicated quickly, as it passes through fewer employees, enabling faster and more effective decision making at a local level. However, managers can find their own productivity falls if they are managing too many people.

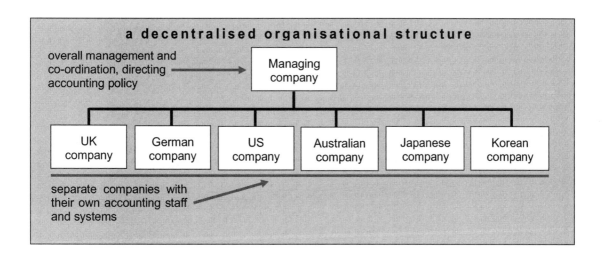

centralised structure – large organisation

A centralised organisation has a series of levels of people, each level controlled by the level above it. This structure – also known as a 'tall' or 'hierarchical' structure – is suitable for a large organisation such as a public limited company or Government Department which may have thousands of employees. In this type of structure, the accounting system will be the responsibility of the Finance Director and is centralised and strictly controlled. Study the diagram on the next page.

In this centralised structure, each manager will be directly responsible for less staff, so has a smaller span of control. This results in more levels of managers and supervisors, so the length of the scalar chain is likely to be long. Decision making will be slowed down as each person will be required to authorise the decision, before passing it 'up the chain' to the next manager. Equally, information will take time to move down from one level to another. However, there will be a very clear 'chain of command', so everyone knows their role in the organisation. As managers are responsible for few reports, their individual productivity will be higher.

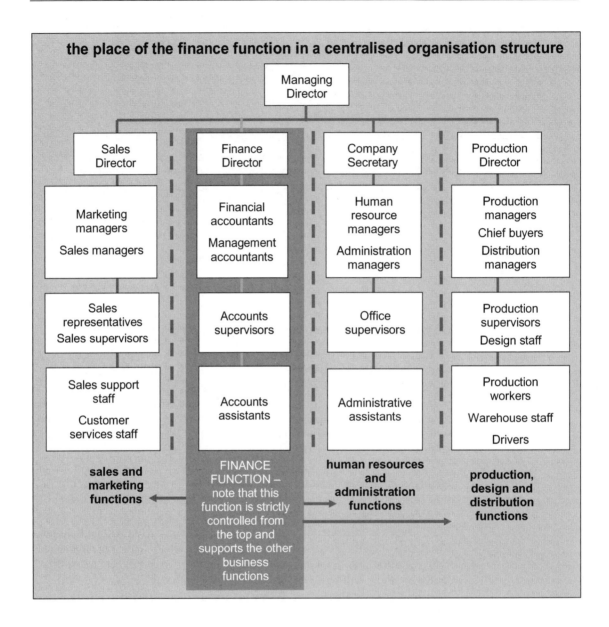

the place of the finance function in a centralised organisation structure

Managing Director

Sales Director	Finance Director	Company Secretary	Production Director
Marketing managers Sales managers	Financial accountants Management accountants	Human resource managers Administration managers	Production managers Chief buyers Distribution managers
Sales representatives Sales supervisors	Accounts supervisors	Office supervisors	Production supervisors Design staff
Sales support staff Customer services staff	Accounts assistants	Administrative assistants	Production workers Warehouse staff Drivers

sales and marketing functions

FINANCE FUNCTION – note that this function is strictly controlled from the top and supports the other business functions

human resources and administration functions

production, design and distribution functions

organisational structure – small business

So far, this chapter has concentrated on large organisations. It is possible that the business provided in the AAT assessment will be a **smaller business** or **voluntary organisation**. The large majority of businesses in the UK are, in fact, small businesses with fifty or fewer employees.

The organisational structure of a small business is more likely to be 'flat' with the boss at the top and a variety of 'functions' or small departments under their direct control.

One of these functions will, of course, be the **accounting function**. This may involve a line manager who oversees a number of assistants and reports directly to the business owner. It may also be the case that the business owner looks after some of the accounting functions, for example negotiating discounts and credit terms with major customers or completing the VAT Return.

This type of business is illustrated in the 'flat structure business' diagram below.

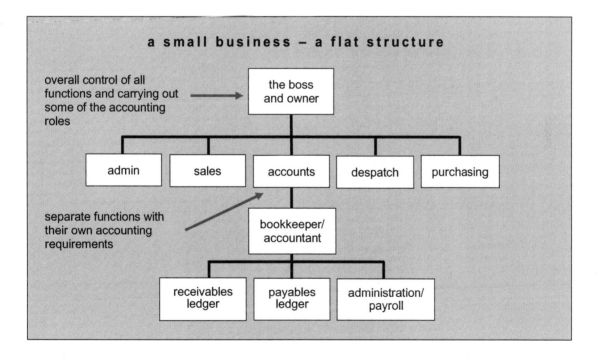

Case
Study

DESIGN FOR LIFE LTD: ORGANISATIONAL STRUCTURE

situation

Have a look back at the material for our example business on pages 10 to 12. Draw the organisational structure for this business.

solution

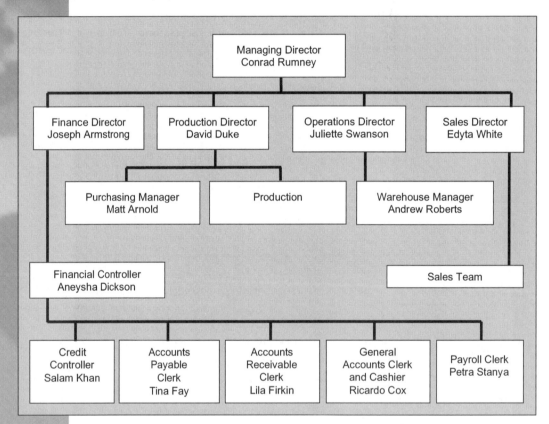

This is a centralised structure, with each Director responsible for their own function.

FUNCTIONS OF AN ACCOUNTING SYSTEM

The assessment requires you to look critically at an existing accounting system and to identify areas for improvement in both the system itself and the way in which it is managed.

A typical accounting system carries out several functions, shown in the diagram below. It is the responsibility of the management to ensure that it operates smoothly.

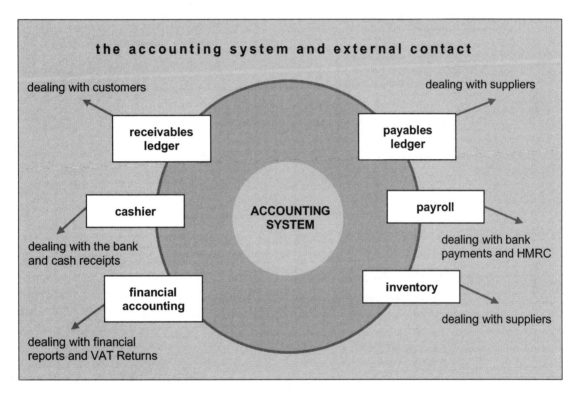

It is important that the accounting system is not seen to operate in isolation. Supporting internal functions in the organisation is just as important as meeting those of the external contacts.

If the organisation is a manufacturing business, these other functions might include production, human resources, sales and marketing and administration.

Study the diagram on the next page to see how the accounting system inter-relates with some of the other internal functions of the organisation.

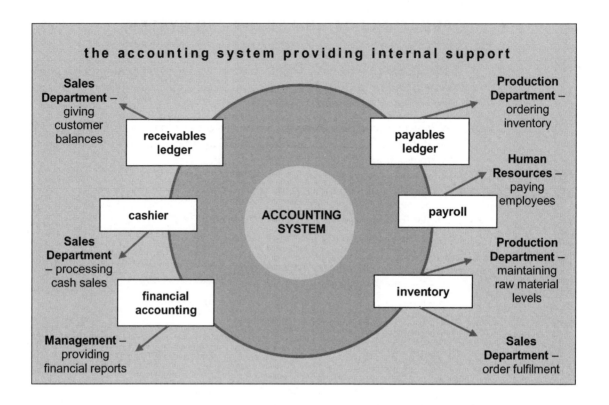

the accounting system providing internal support

Sales Department – giving customer balances

receivables ledger

Production Department – ordering inventory

Human Resources – paying employees

cashier

ACCOUNTING SYSTEM

payables ledger

payroll

Sales Department – processing cash sales

Production Department – maintaining raw material levels

financial accounting

inventory

Management – providing financial reports

Sales Department – order fulfilment

Answering the assessment

When you evaluate any accounting system you will need to analyse the way in which the accounting system supports the rest of the organisation and its external contacts.

Your analysis might consider weaknesses in the way the system is structured, in the way it is managed and in the way in which it communicates with people – eg customers or suppliers – **outside** the organisation.

Your analysis should also look at the way in which the accounting system deals with other functions **inside** the organisation. A good starting point is to look at communications between the various departments. Are there any weaknesses, or deficiencies, at all?

THE NEED FOR GOOD COMMUNICATION

lines of communication in an accounting system

You will need to consider the effectiveness of the communication between people in the accounting function itself – in addition to the communication between people in other functions, eg sales.

The diagram below illustrates the lines of communication between accounting employees in a large company. The accounting system here is subdivided into the areas of financial and management accounting.

The boxes with the dark grey background all represent specific accounting roles. You will see that the structure is set out in a series of layers of authority and responsibility.

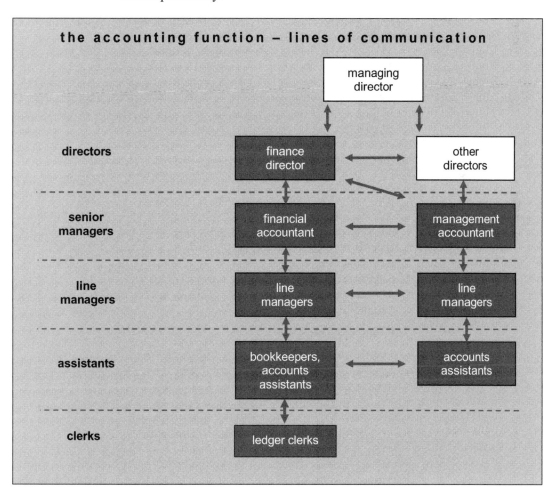

the accounting function – lines of communication

CONTROL OF RESOURCES BY INDIVIDUALS IN THE ORGANISATION

the need for resources

Adequate **resources** are essential to the functioning of an organisation. All come at a cost. Resources can be classified under four main headings:

■ **equipment and material resources**

These include premises in which to work and equipment needed on a day-to-day basis. They also include the materials that may be used – raw materials, inventory and consumables such as pens and photocopy paper. A car manufacturer will clearly have a greater need for equipment and material resources in a factory than a firm of insurance brokers working from a town centre office. The important point here is that in both cases the resources will need to be adequate.

■ **human resources**

This term is used widely to describe the 'people' function in organisations. There is always a need for the right number of appropriately skilled people to work within an organisation, whether in a management or an operational role.

■ **information**

This is an essential resource and must be readily available to whoever needs it within the organisation. Computer-based systems with up-to-date and accurate information are the ideal solution. Information in a manufacturing or retail business, for example, will include product specifications, prices, inventory levels, customer orders and supplier orders. A travel agency will need different types of information, but equally, the data will need to be accurate and up to date. The impact of technology on accounting systems is covered in more detail in Chapter 5.

■ **financial resources**

This term means 'money' which is either available currently or can be made available within a set time period to allow spending in line with a particular budget allocation. This is probably the most critical type of resource for the functioning of the organisation. It affects all areas.

control of resources by individuals

As part of the assessment, you could consider which individuals within the organisation control the supply of the various resources described above and whether it is appropriate or not. Control of resources is normally dictated by the various levels of budget within an organisation.

For example, the production or staffing budget of a business is likely to be decided upon at director level and the departmental budget will be the responsibility of the departmental manager. Line managers (supervisors) will also have decisions to make about control of resources – for example, they may be given the power to allow the staff to work overtime and to order small items of office equipment. Employees at assistant level will also have control of resources at a reduced level, for example ordering stationery items or tea and coffee for the rest room. It is all a question of which level of management that an employee is in the organisation and how large the overall organisation is, ie its scale.

The diagram below sets out the hierarchy of individuals who will make decisions about controlling resources; it shows 'level' and 'scale'.

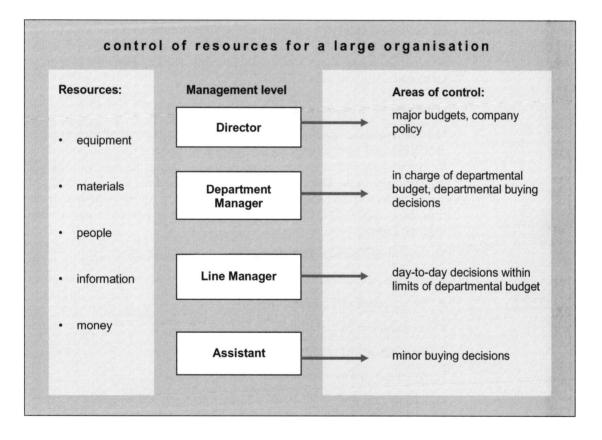

errors and fraud within the accounting system

The control of resources brings with it the opportunity both for error and for fraud. Both can be avoided with the enforcement of reviewing and monitoring procedures.

Error includes situations involving over-ordering of materials – for example, ordering 5,000 suspension files instead of 100 where the units ordered were boxes of 50 rather than individual files.

Fraud is a fact of life where control of resources is concerned. It can range from a director siphoning off funds by 'fiddling the books' to the supposedly innocent pilfering of stationery at assistant level. The issue of fraud is covered in detail in Chapter 4.

FINANCIAL ACCOUNTS AND MANAGEMENT ACCOUNTS

When reviewing an accounting system, you should always consider whether the business is able to produce the accounting information it needs in a timely and accurate manner. This information could be either in the form of financial accounts or management account information. The key elements of each of these are considered below.

financial accounts

Most organisations produce Financial Accounts at the end of each year, to enable external users to understand the performance and financial position of the business. In the case of a limited company, this is the legal or statutory responsibility of the Directors. During the year, the financial transactions of the business are recorded by the accounts team. At the year-end, these financial transactions in the business are presented in a set of accounts in the required format.

The key financial statements that are usually produced are:

- the statement of profit or loss
- the statement of financial position
- the statement of cash flows
- the statement of changes in equity

Financial statements are produced:

- for **internal use** by the organisation for planning and budgeting reasons
- for **external use** to provide information to stakeholders such as banks, shareholders, suppliers, customers, employees, possible investors and Government bodies such as HMRC.

The Level 4 Unit Drafting and Interpreting Financial Statements shows how to produce company accounts and what they include in detail.

management accounts

Management accounts use the same transactional data to produce information for internal use to allow the directors and managers to control and manage the business. This information is often produced on a daily, weekly or monthly basis, in any format the business requires, to help those who read it to understand the financial implications of decisions they are making. It can be looking at the recent past or considering future decisions.

For example, a budget may be produced at the start of the year to help managers plan resources, production schedules and prices. During the year managers may be monitored against this budget and variances calculated to see whether the business needs to adjust its plans due to changes in the market or economy. A forecast may be prepared based on performance to date to assist in the decision making process. In Chapter 3, we will look at the types of report that managers and other internal stakeholders may need.

COMPLYING WITH REGULATION AND LEGISLATION

Complying with regulation and legislation is very important for a business. If it does not comply, it could become liable to fines or legal action. The accounts department will be structured to ensure the staff who may be affected by such regulations and legislation are able to monitor them and make appropriate changes when needed, to maintain compliance.

For example, the Financial Accountant will be responsible for monitoring compliance with Accounting Standards, part of the Level 4 Unit Drafting and Interpreting Financial Statements, which we mentioned earlier.

The Payroll Clerk will be trained in the latest tax regulations, set out in the Finance Act, to ensure Income Tax, National Insurance and other statutory deductions are deducted correctly from individuals and paid on time to HMRC. The Accounts Receivables Clerk will know which sales attract VAT and at what rate.

Changes may be required because of the introduction of new external regulations or changes to existing rules (for example, a change in VAT rate).

Whatever the case, the accounting system should be able to react to any external changes and have the internal policies and procedures established and in hand, in order to be able to deal with them. Examples include:

- **changes in accounting terminology and accounting standards**

  You will know from your studies that there is move away from UK GAAP accounting terminology to international terminology which has been established by the International Accounting Standards Board (IASB) through to International Accounting Standards and International Financial

Reporting Standards. These are currently applicable to larger limited companies in the UK. It is likely that this terminology will eventually supersede the existing UK GAAP terminology, meaning that more and more organisations over time will need to refer to 'trade receivables' rather than 'debtors' and to 'inventory' rather than to 'stock'.

Organisations will need to amend much documentation and invest in staff training to cope with these changes. Again, internal policies and procedures will need to be established to deal with this.

- **a change in the VAT rate**

This can seriously disturb the smooth running of any VAT-registered business. It particularly affects retail businesses, involving the repricing of goods on the shelf and in the warehouse, reprinting of catalogues, amendments on the website, amendments to invoicing software and the training of staff to deal with a confused public. The accounting functions affected most would be accounts receivable, accounts payable and cash book.

Most large retailers will have internal policies and procedures to deal with this situation, as the VAT rate can change with each new Finance Act.

Chapter Summary

- The organisational structure will influence how the accounting system will be set up. Decentralised (flat) structures will have autonomous companies with separate accounts departments, which may include few staff – eg Accounts Receivable Ledger, Accounts Payable Ledger, Accountant. Centralised (hierarchical) structures may have thousands of employees and several types of accounting employees eg Accounts Clerks, Accounts Assistants and Accounts Managers.

- The nature of the business determines which functions the accounting department carry out eg payroll, sales, cashier.

- Each function will support different areas of the business eg Accounts Receivable will give information to Sales, Payroll will liaise with Human Resources.

- Good communication is vital for the accounts department to collect and deal with the information needed to produce accurate, timely financial information. Accounts will deal with all departments in the organisation to allow them to do this.

- Resources allow the business to meet its needs and objectives and can include equipment, people, information and finance.

- Financial statements are produced using the accounting systems by the directors, primarily for external users.

- Financial statements usually include a statement of profit or loss, statement of financial position and statement of cash flows.

- Management accounts are only for internal use and may be in any format the business needs. They are produced using the same information used for the financial statements. Information may be produced daily, weekly or monthly.

- External regulations, including legislation, need to be complied with and the accounting function ensures this by including this responsibility within specific job roles. For example, Payroll staff are knowledgeable in Income Tax rules, Accounts Receivable ledger staff in VAT rules and the Finance Director in Accounting Standards.

- When external regulations, such as accounting standards and the Finance Act, change, this may require the accounts department to make changes to its working practices to ensure the business continues to comply with them. The relevant staff will be responsible for ensuring the changes are made.

<table>
<tr><td rowspan="8">**Key Terms**</td></tr>
</table>

organisational structure	how the different parts of a business are organised and report to each other, eg decentralised (flat) or centralised (hierarchical)
span of control	how many employees report to a manager
length of scalar chain	the number of levels in a company from the top to the bottom
functions in accounts	the activities undertaken in accounts to produce the financial information the business needs and record the financial transactions of the business – eg Payroll, Accounts Payable Ledger, Accounts Receivable Ledger
financial accounts	a set of financial statements, including statement of profit or loss, statement of financial position and statement of cash flows, produced in regulated format for internal and external use
management accounts	information produced using the accounting systems for internal use, to allow the staff to plan, monitor and control activity within the business in any format that management wishes
external regulations	regulations that need to be complied with by the business for it to operate efficiently and effectively – eg VAT rates, included in the Finance Act and International Accounting Standards. If the organisation does not follow these it may be subject to fines and legal action

Activities

2.1 Who has the statutory duty to prepare accounts for a limited company? Tick the appropriate options below.

(a)	The company's auditors ✗	
(b)	The directors of the company	✓
(c)	The Chief Accountant	
(d)	Companies House ✗	

2.2 Which of the following statements about a wide span of control is true or false? Tick the correct choice for each statement.

		True	False
(a)	It is more expensive to operate		✓
(b)	It improves productivity for the organisation		✓
(c)	It has more levels of management		✓
(d)	Decision making is faster	✓	

2.3 Watkins Recruitment Limited is a firm specialising in providing recruitment services for its clients based in Berkshire and London. It is run by the two owners, William Watkins and Harry Watkins, who employ fifteen staff, including one who is responsible for accounts within the business. They are internet-based, hiring meeting rooms when needed on an ad-hoc basis to meet candidates or clients.

(a) List the main activities Watkins Recruitment Limited would have to account for and the main accounting functions.

(b) What type of structure would you expect Watkins Recruitment Limited to have and why?

2.4   Footy for Fun Limited is a manufacturer of table football games. It has two divisions, one of which manufactures a range of quality products, from standalone tables to small games you can put onto an ordinary table and play. This division sells to high street retailers and internet distributors. The other division designs and makes custom football tables, which are sold all over the world and made to order. Both divisions are based in a factory in St Albans and the business employs 400 people.

(a)   Identify the main activities Footy for Fun Limited would have to account for and the main accounting functions.

(b)   What type of organisational structure would you expect Footy for Fun Limited to have and why?

2.5   Train Travel Limited runs a train operating company delivering travel in Surrey, Sussex, Kent and Hampshire. It has been operating for several years and employs several thousand people. The Finance Act has recently changed the rates wages are taxed at, the tax free allowances available and also employees are now taxed on the entire value of any travel discounts they might have as part of their employment as if they were a wage payment. Some discounts are of considerable value for Train Travel Limited's employees. The business has a dedicated Payroll Team, run by a Payroll Manager.

(a)   What type of organisational structure do you think Train Travel Limited might have and why?

(b)   Draft an email from the Payroll Manager to the Payroll Team, copying in the Finance Director and the Human Resources Manager, stating what changes might be needed to ensure the business continues to comply with payroll legislation.

2.6   If there was a change in VAT which was not implemented, who would be held responsible by HMRC?

(a)	The Finance Director	
(b)	The Sales Director	
(c)	The Managing Director	
(d)	All of the Directors	✔

3 Stakeholders and their information needs

this chapter covers...

In this chapter we examine the different stakeholders of the business, both external and internal, and the type of information they may wish to use in order to keep informed of the way in which the business is performing and being run.

The areas the chapter covers include:

- *the different types of stakeholders, both external and internal*

- *how the management information is designed to fit the needs of the business*

- *the types of information stakeholders might use, including financial statements, management accounts and budgetary reporting*

- *the calculation of performance indicators (ratios)*

- *the importance of ethics and sustainability when producing information for stakeholders*

STAKEHOLDERS – EXTERNAL AND INTERNAL

A stakeholder is a person or organisation that has an 'interest' in another organisation.

Stakeholders can be internal (eg employees, managers, shareholders who run the business) or external (eg shareholders who are not running the business, banks, customers, suppliers, the tax authorities and the general public). Let us look at external stakeholders initially.

Take for example a retail organisation such as an electrical retail chain which is also a public limited company quoted on the stock market.

The functioning of the accounting system will be affected by external stakeholders in a number of ways:

- **customers** will need to be provided with easy and efficient means of making payment, and in suitable circumstances, credit terms and finance

- **suppliers** will need to be paid on time and credit terms and discounts will need to be negotiated and administered

- **banks** that are lending money to the company are likely to require regular (eg monthly) management accounts, eg levels of sales, inventory, cash held, payables, receivables

- **the tax authorities** (HM Revenue & Customs – a Government Department) will require calculation and payment of Corporation Tax, Value Added Tax and collection of Income Tax and National Insurance through the PAYE system

- **shareholders (the owners)** who do not run the business will require information about the financial performance of the company in the form of an annual financial report downloadable from the company's website

- **trade associations** will request financial statistics such as sales trends, details of exports, wage rates and so on for their regular trade reports

- the **general public** will be a stakeholder in the business, if it is a public limited company, as the business is likely to employ many people and affect the local or national economy if it got into financial difficulties

The relationship of an organisation with its external stakeholders is shown in the diagram set out on the next page.

Stakeholders can also be internal to the business:

- employees will want to know how well the business is performing and therefore if their jobs are likely to be secure in the future. If they have bonus-related pay, they will want information to help them work out if they are likely to be paid the bonus at the end of each bonus period eg weekly, monthly or yearly

■ managers will need to be given information to allow them to manage the business effectively. For example, sales figures by branch could help them decide which branches are performing well and which need to improve. If branch staff are paid partly by bonus, performance information would be very important to them as well

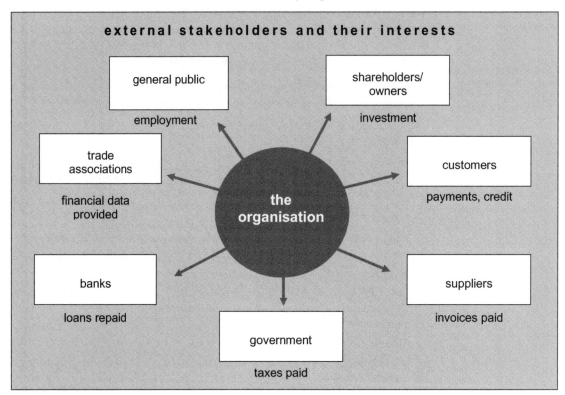

external stakeholders and their interests

general public — employment

shareholders/owners — investment

trade associations — financial data provided

customers — payments, credit

banks — loans repaid

the organisation

government — taxes paid

suppliers — invoices paid

Case
Study

COMFORTABLE KENNELS

situation

Florence and Rebecca Carter have run 'Comfortable Kennels' for several years. They cater for dogs whose owners go on holiday for up to a month, marketing the kennels as 'a home from home'. They have looked after many of the same animals for several years and have a good working relationship with the local vet. Food and other essentials are supplied by a local pet store and delivered weekly.

They have recently invested in some new kennels (with large exercise areas attached), securing funding from the local branch of the Black Pony Bank. They have also taken on two new staff, now employing eight in total.

required

Identify the main internal and external stakeholders of Comfortable Kennels and explain why they are important.

solution

The main internal stakeholders are Florence and Rebecca, as they not only own but also run the kennels, along with the eight staff they employ. They are interested in how well the business is run and how profitable it is, as they want to have long-term security of their earnings.

There are several external stakeholders:

- The customers are interested, as they want the kennels to continue to provide a service for their dogs, some of which are old and may not like to go to a new kennels.

- The vet will want the business to be successful so Comfortable Kennels will continue to be a customer and they can provide vet services to it in the future.

- The local pet store will also want the business to continue to trade so they can also continue to sell to it.

- HMRC will want to verify the business is paying the correct tax liabilities, ie payroll, VAT and Income Tax.

- Finally, the bank will be concerned with the financial performance of the business. It needs to be confident that it is likely to receive all the finance charges and repayments for the loan.

MANAGEMENT INFORMATION

management information systems (MIS)

A large organisation is often served by a **management information system (MIS).** This is a computer-based system which provides up-to-date, accurate and relevant information to management. An efficient MIS will enable management to make informed decisions promptly.

By 'management' we mean all levels of management, from line managers (supervisors) through to the Finance Director. Clearly the type and level of information required will vary according to the role of the manager and the type of decision expected of that manager. Examples of the type of data produced by an accounting MIS include:

- sales figures for products and regions

- inventory levels

- customer account details, ranging from balances to detailed reports such as the Aged Receivables Analysis

- budgetary control reports showing variances

- profitability reports by product

You will see from this range of information that decision making can range from 'Do we allow this customer any more credit?' through to 'Do we continue to manufacture this product?'.

INTERNAL STAKEHOLDERS AND THEIR INFORMATION NEEDS

management accounts and budgetary controls

Many organisations use management information systems to produce monthly management accounts, in any format that seems appropriate for their managers to use. An example of a layout of a set of management accounts is given below:

Modern Machinery Limited

Management Accounts for the month of October 20-1

	Flexed budget		Actual		Variance
Volume (units)	2,600,000		2,600,000		
	£000		£000		£000
Revenue		13,000		14,300	1,300 F
Expenses:					
Material	2,080		1,950		130 F
Labour	2,340		2,392		52 A
Power	1,690		1,768		78 A
Storage	966		992		26 A
Transport	1,430		1,410		20 F
Maintenance	770		790		20 A
Depreciation	970		960		10 F
Admin expenses	650		658		8 A
Total expenses		10,896		10,920	24 A
Operating profit		2,104		3,380	1,276 F

By breaking the business down into different expense and income areas, the management information system can enable the business to monitor performance against budget. You may have covered this already in some detail if you have studied the Level 4 Applied Management Accounting unit.

Looking at the management accounts on the previous page, there are some variances which management would be likely to investigate, such as the power and material variances, as the others may be less significant.

In another business, the budgetary reports could be more based around sales, contribution and profitability. The MIS system will be designed to ensure this information can be extracted easily. The next Case Study illustrates this.

Case Study

PRETTY POTTERY LIMITED: BUDGETARY CONTROL REPORT

situation

Pretty Pottery Limited is a small business, based in Ledbury, producing handmade pottery vases for sale in the local area and directly via the internet. It does not currently use standard costing. The following report has been produced, comparing actual results to a flexed budget. The original budget was for 5,000 units and the actual units sold were 6,500.

Flexed Budget Operating Statement 6,500 units

	Budget £	Actual £	Variance £
Sales	487,500	495,000	7,500F
Less: Cost of sales			
Materials	97,500	112,000	14,500A
Labour	65,000	97,500	32,500A
Production overheads	47,000	55,000	8,000A
Cost of sales	209,500	264,500	55,000A
Gross profit	278,000	230,500	47,500A
Admin & selling overheads	25,000	27,000	2,000A
Distribution overheads	45,000	51,000	6,000A
Operating profit	208,000	152,500	55,500A

required

Comment on any issues highlighted by the budget report that the management of Pretty Pottery Limited should be made aware of. You can support your answer with additional calculations.

solution

The following additional calculations would be appropriate:

Additional calculations	Budget	Actual
Average sales price per unit	= 487,500/6,500 units = £75.00	= 495,000/6,500 = £76.15
Gross profit percentage = Gross profit/ sales x 100	= 278,000/487,500x 100 = 57.0%	= 230,500/495,000 x 100 = 46.6%
Operating profit percentage = Operating profit/sales x 100	= 208,000/487,500 x 100 = 42.7%	= 152,500/495,000 x 100 = 30.8%

Pretty Pottery Limited can see how the reduced gross profit percentage has eroded the operating profit percentage.

The actual selling price was £1.15 per unit higher than budget, so the increased cost of sales for materials, labour and production overheads, shown by the adverse variances, all reduce the gross profit percentage. This would be an area that management should monitor more closely in future, perhaps weekly or monthly, to drive up profits, as the variances on labour, material and production overhead are significant and indicate a lack of control.

Non-production overheads are also over-budget, reducing the reduced operating profit margin further.

This analysis assumes that the original budget was sound.

changes to MIS as an organisation grows

Often when a business is set up, it will start using a very simple MIS – perhaps only a simple set of general ledger codes – and produce management accounts periodically. However, as it grows its information needs will change and so the systems will need to be amended or replaced to enable the business to access the information it needs.

For example, a family that runs one furniture store will need information on sales, type of product sold, wages and monthly management accounts. However, if they decide to open several stores around the country, they would need more information to allow them to budget, monitor and control the different locations. The MIS would need to be able to generate information such as gross profit margin by product, staff costs by department and store, and profitability by store so they could run the business as effectively as possible.

financial statements for internal use

Financial statements – and the **ratios** that can be extracted from them – provide management with information about the financial state of the organisation. They will enable management to analyse past performance and also, in the **master budget**, project future performance.

Areas of particular interest to senior management include:

statement of profit or loss	• sales performance
	• gross and net profit margins
	• comparison of areas of expense
statement of financial position	• liquidity
	• gearing
	• return on capital employed
statement of changes in equity	• financing by share issues
	• level of dividend payments
	• impact of asset revaluations
statement of cash flows	• explanation of changes in the cash position of a company
	• investments made in assets
	• all sources of financing

EXTERNAL STAKEHOLDERS AND THEIR INFORMATION NEEDS

The information available to external stakeholders will most commonly be the financial statements. This information may be audited, depending on the size of the business and whether the business or stakeholders believe it to be appropriate. The audit is performed independently of management and gives an opinion as to whether the accounts are accurate and give a true and fair view of the business at the reporting date.

If a small business which falls below audit thresholds is applying for a new bank loan, it is possible the bank will request a set of audited financial statements to support the loan application.

Other information may also be requested. For example:

■ **Banks**

When lending, banks need to assess the financial performance and financial strength of an organisation. They need to make sure that any lending can be repaid and also that there are sufficient assets available for security. They will want to see:

- a statement of profit or loss to check that profit is being generated

- a statement of financial position to ensure that a company is not over-geared (ie there is not too much borrowing already in relation to equity)

- a cash budget to confirm that the company will have adequate cash flow over the next twelve months (note that a 'cash budget' is not the same as a 'statement of cash flows')

■ **Suppliers**

The credit control function of many suppliers requires sight of the accounts of prospective customers – either directly or through credit reference agencies – so that they can carry out ratio analysis before granting credit terms.

■ **HM Revenue & Customs**

The statement of profit or loss will provide the source of the data for the calculation of tax due on profits made.

■ **Shareholders and investors**

The published financial statements of public limited companies contain the statement of profit or loss, statement of financial position, statement of changes in equity and the statement of cash flows. These and the investment ratios they provide enable owners of shares and prospective investors to assess the return they are likely to make on the company shares.

The stakeholder may then use this information to calculate performance indicators, or ratios, to determine how well the business is performing and how financially stable it is. You may already have covered ratios in your studies in the Drafting and Interpreting Financial Statements Unit. However, as it is such an important area, the Case Study that follows sets out how to calculate the key ratios which a stakeholder may look at.

Case
Study

TRENDY TOGS LIMITED

situation

Trendy Togs Limited has a unique range of clothing, selling via shops in London, Birmingham, Manchester and Edinburgh. It began to expand rapidly in 20-2 and opened two new shops. It has also started to sell via the internet to other clothes shops and offers 30 days credit. It wishes to continue to expand and is looking for additional finance in the form of a bank loan.

Trendy Togs Ltd

Statement of Profit or Loss for the year ended 31 December 20-2

	£000
Revenue	6,528
Cost of sales	3,256
Gross profit	3,272
Administrative expenses	954
Selling and distribution costs	321
Operating profit	1,997
Finance costs	100
Profit before taxation	1,897
Taxation	258
Profit after taxation	1,639

Trendy Togs Ltd

Statement of Financial Position as at 31 December 20-2

ASSETS	£000
Non-current assets	16,263
Current assets:	
Inventories	240
Trade receivables	97
Cash and cash equivalents	478
	815
Total assets	17,078
EQUITY AND LIABILITIES	
Equity	
Ordinary share capital (£1 shares)	9,604
Retained earnings	4,862
Total equity	14,466
Non-current liabilities	2,000
Current liabilities	
Trade payables	354
Tax liabilities	258
	612
Total liabilities	2,612
Total equity and liabilities	17,078

required

(a) Calculate appropriate performance indicators (ratios) for the bank to consider.

(b) State with reasons whether you would or you would not give them a loan.

solution

(a)

Ratio Analysis	20-2	Performance indicator 20-2	Workings
Gross profit margin (Gross margin)	50.12%	Gross margin %	Gross profit / revenue * 100 = 3,272/6,528*100 50.12%
Operating profit margin (Operating margin)	30.59%	Operating profit %	Operating profit / revenue x 100 = 1,997/6,528*100 30.59%
ROCE (Return on capital employed)	12.13%	ROCE %	Operating profit / (Total equity + non-current liabilities) * 100 = 1,997/(14,466+2,000)*100 12.13%
Gearing	12.15%	Gearing %	= Non-current liabilities / (Non-current liabilities + Total equity) x 100 = 2,000/(2,000+14,466) 12.15%
Current ratio (Working capital ratio)	1.33:1	Current ratio	= Current assets / Current liabilities = 815/612 1.33:1
'Acid test' ratio (Quick ratio)	0.94:1	Acid test/ Quick ratio	= (Current assets – inventories) / Current liabilities = (815-240)/612 0.94:1
Inventory turnover	13.6 times	Inventory turnover	= Cost of sales / inventories = 3,256 / 240 13.57 times
Inventory holding period (days)	26.9 days	Inventory holding period	= Inventory / cost of sales * 365 = 240/3,256*365 26.90
Trade receivables (debtors) collection period (days)	5.4 days	Trade receivables collection period	Trade receivables / Revenue * 365 = 97/6,528*365 5.42
Trade payables (creditors) payment period (days)	39.7 days	Trade payables payment period	Trade payables / cost of sales * 365 = 354/3,256*365 39.68

(b) Trendy Togs Limited has very low gearing at the moment and strong operating and gross profit margins. The current and acid test ratios are reasonable, given the type of industry Trendy Togs Limited operates in.

Given the high profitability, low gearing and good level of liquidity, the bank is likely to give Trendy Togs Limited a loan on good terms.

MAINTAINING RELATIONSHIPS WITH THE STAKEHOLDERS

ethical considerations

Often stakeholders, such as employees, banks, customers and suppliers, enjoy a relationship with an organisation for many years and will request and receive a variety of information over that time.

Any information regarding the company, whether it is the weekly sales figures or the year end accounts, must be produced and distributed under ethical principles, by which accountants are bound.

The principle ethical considerations, which you have already studied at Level 3, are set out below.

- **Objectivity** – decisions based on facts, not influenced by other people

- **Integrity** – straightforward and honest dealings with people

- **Professional Behaviour** – complying with the rules and regulations that govern the accounting profession, as well as legislation, including upholding the profession's reputation

- **Professional Competence and Due Care** – having the right level of skill, working carefully, thoroughly and to deadlines and declining work when you are not able to perform it

- **Confidentiality** – not disclosing information obtained due to work to third parties

We will now cover these fundamental ethical principles in more detail, along with some practical examples.

objectivity

A person who is objective is a person who sticks to the facts and does not allow his or her decisions or actions to be affected by other people's opinions or influence. Objectivity can be threatened by:

- a conflict of interest – a situation where professional judgement is affected because the employee could benefit personally from a transaction

■ undue influence – a situation where someone is putting undue pressure on you to do something that you do not consider professional or ethical

For example, an Assistant Accountant has found out that his immediate boss, the Accounts Manager, takes his wife to Paris on company expenses. The Accounts Manager asks the Assistant Accountant to keep quiet about it, in return for promising to recommend him for promotion.

Similarly, Accounts Payable staff may be asked by the Finance Director to delay supplier payments to improve the cash position of the company at the end of the financial year – this is known as 'window dressing'. This may be against supplier credit terms but, as the Accounts Payable staff report to the Finance Director, they may feel they have to do it, even if it means causing cash flow problems for their suppliers.

integrity

Employees who act with 'integrity' are:

■ straightforward – they obey the rules

■ honest – they do not cover up the truth, fiddle the books, or allow anything to pass through the accounting system which they know has not been checked

■ fair dealing – they treat everyone on an equal basis; they are not involved in 'shady' deals

■ truthful – they do not tell lies, falsify or 'fudge' figures, or mislead customers and suppliers with false information, eg prices, discounts

In short, that person will not allow anything that is incorrect or misleading to pass through the accounting system or be given to stakeholders. The principle of integrity applies equally to major and minor breaches of ethics.

For example, if the Chief Accountant was deliberately adjusting sales to avoid paying out bonuses to sales staff at the end of the year, breaching the integrity ethic, the trust built up between the employee and the employer would be harmed. The employees might take legal action against the organisation, or they may either leave or behave in a similar way to management, making fraud (covered in Chapter 4) more likely.

If a stakeholder, such as a bank, were to find out information provided to them had been adjusted for any reason, this could result in loan funding being withdrawn. This would have a damaging impact on the long-term future of the business.

professional behaviour

Professional behaviour is the individual complying with the rules and regulations that govern the accounting profession, including upholding the profession's reputation.

The type of rules and regulations might include:

■ accounting standards

■ the ethical code

Areas where an accountant may damage the profession's reputations are:

■ ignoring requests for information or producing information late

■ using abusive language with other staff either directly or in emails

For example, the Credit Controller has decided to handle late payers by 'naming and shaming' them on the company website. This behaviour is likely to alienate customers quickly and damage the reputation of the business, as well as the accounting profession.

Similarly, when the Financial Controller knowingly incorrectly records a significant repair as a non-current asset, to make the profit look better in the financial statements, not only are they acting without integrity, they are also behaving very unprofessionally.

professional competence and due care

Professional Competence means achieving a level of knowledge and skills needed for working at a particular level in the workplace. The more senior the employee, the greater the knowledge and skills that will be needed to perform the work.

Due Care means that the accounting employee must take the required level of care appropriate to the task that is being done. In other words the accounting employee must provide a competent and 'professional' service.

Professional Competence and Due Care require that the accounting employee should:

■ act diligently – this means carrying out a task according to instructions, carefully, thoroughly and on time

■ use sound judgement in applying professional knowledge

■ know when to refuse to carry out an area of work (eg payroll processing) if the employee does not have the necessary knowledge or skills

■ plan career progression through CPD (Continuing Professional Development), a programme of qualifications, internal courses and expanding experience

For example, an accounts line manager has been asked to be responsible for the Payroll Section for a few months to cover maternity leave. They have no real experience of this area of the accounting system, but agree to the request because they are looking for promotion. They are not professionally competent to perform this task.

An Accounts Manager is preparing some financial figures for a company board meeting. They are going away on holiday that night, so hurry through the figures and miss updating two key tables. They have not taken due care.

confidentiality

Confidentiality within an Accounting Department is the duty not to disclose information held by the organisation about another person or organisation to anyone else, unless permission has been given.

The type of information that should not be given to outsiders includes personal or business details of:

■ customers and clients

■ suppliers

■ colleagues

■ internal information about the organisation

'Outsiders' who should not be given information include:

■ family members

■ social acquaintances

■ 'cold callers', eg marketing survey companies

For example, a Payroll Manager tells his friend, the Accounts Manager, exactly how much the Financial Controller currently earns. The Financial Controller is leaving and the Accounts Manager wants to apply for the position. The Payroll Manager is clearly breaking confidentiality here.

sustainability

As part of your previous studies, you will have considered sustainability. However, to remind you, the definition of sustainability is as follows:

> **'Sustainability is development that meets the needs of the present without compromising the ability of future generations to meet their own needs.'**

There are three main principles of sustainability:

■ economic or corporate growth – decisions are based on the long-term, not the short-term, growth of the business

■ environmental protection – decisions made do not harm the environment

■ social equality – decisions promote the well-being of all employees and the local community

These are sometimes referred to as 'profit, planet and people' – the triple bottom line – and set out below are some examples for each objective.

economic growth

- using fair pricing policies when charging customers

- paying a fair wage, rather than the lowest possible, to allow workers to remain with the business in the long-term and protect its future

environmental protection

- reducing the carbon footprint of a business eg cycle to work schemes, car sharing

- using suppliers who promote sustainable practices in the production of their products

social equality

- sponsorship of local charity events

- employing local labour where possible or training local people to become more skilled and employable

---

Answering the assessment

In the assessment, you will consider ethics and sustainability both in terms of policies and practices the business currently has and also potential improvements it could make to promote more ethical and sustainable practices.

Chapter Summary

- There are many different stakeholders who could be interested in a business, both internal and external, including employees and managers, banks, customers, suppliers, and HMRC.

- The organisation needs to produce information for these stakeholders using a management information system (MIS).

- The MIS will be specifically designed to meet the needs of the business in which it operates. For example, a retail organisation would collect information on sales by product and location, comparing budgeted to actual results.

- The MIS will provide the business with the right information to allow it to calculate performance indicators, to assist in running the business and monitoring key areas.

- Within an organisation, budgetary reports and management reports will be created to fit the needs of the managers and employees.

- External stakeholders are likely to be given the financial statements, which they can use for carrying out ratio analysis. This will give an indication of the financial performance and position of the business.

- Accountants are bound by ethics and sustainable principles when providing information to stakeholders. Information provided must comply with those principles and be delivered in a timely and appropriate manner.

Key Terms

stakeholder	a person or organisation that has an 'interest' in another organisation
internal stakeholder	managers and employees who are employed by a business. This could include directors in a large company
external stakeholder	a person or organisation who is connected but not involved in the day-to-day running of the business, eg banks, customers, suppliers
management information system	a computer-based system which provides up-to-date, accurate and relevant information to management
performance indicator	a quantifiable measure used to evaluate the success of an organisation in meeting its objectives for performance
ratio analysis	analysis of the financial statements, often performed by external stakeholders, to evaluate and assess performance and financial stability
ethical principles	the principles by which accountants are bound and under which they must produce accurate, reliable and relevant information
sustainable principles	how a business meets the needs of the present without compromising the ability of future generations to meet their own needs, in terms of economic growth, environmental protection and social equality

Activities

3.1 Speedy Car Services Limited fits tyres, brakes, batteries and exhausts at fifteen branches around the Midlands. It carries many of these items in stock and uses one main supplier, which delivers them daily and can provide more specialist items when needed.

Speedy Car Services Limited has been trading for several years and employs 130 people, most of whom have been with the company for several years. The branches operate a bonus system for the employees, based on the sales figures for each branch.

Two years ago, the business invested in three new branches as well as improved diagnostic equipment for various makes of car. This investment was funded by a five year loan from the bank. The business is owned by three members of the same family, who all work at one of the main branches.

(a) Identify the key stakeholders of the business, both internal and external, and explain why they are important. Give examples of information the stakeholders may wish to look at.

(b) Give examples of some possible performance indicators and information to include on budgetary control reports, to assist the owners in running the business.

3.2 Almost Vintage Limited makes and sells copies of 1950's style vintage clothing to retailers across the globe. It is a well-established business, employing ten people, who use quality fabrics and today's sewing methods to create replica clothing. The business is owned by Narita Stanley.

It has an excellent reputation amongst its customers and many place several orders per year. The usual credit terms offered are 30 days, with some preferred customers being given 45 days. It has very few bad debts.

The fabrics used for the clothing are produced to order in France and Italy by three or four key fabric printers.

(a) Identify the key stakeholders of the business, both internal and external, and explain why they are important. Give examples of information the stakeholders may wish to look at.

(b) Give examples of some possible performance indicators and information to include in budgetary control reports, to assist the owners in running the business.

3.3   Plum Limited manufactures specialist gas detection equipment. The financial statements are set out below:

Statement of profit or loss for the year ended 31 December 20-6

	£000
Revenue	36,000
Cost of sales	(20,800)
Gross profit	15,200
Operating expenses	(13,310)
Operating profit	1,890
Finance costs	(175)
Profit before tax	1,715
Tax	(849)
Profit for the period	866

Statement of financial position at 31 December 20-6

	£000
ASSETS	
Non-current assets	
Property, plant and equipment	25,708
	25,708
Current assets	
Inventories	2,736
Trade receivables	3,960
Cash and cash equivalents	757
	7,453
Total assets	33,161
EQUITY AND LIABILITIES	
Equity	
Ordinary share capital (£1 shares)	11,000
Retained earnings	15,950
Total equity	26,950
Non-current liabilities	
Bank loans	3,500
	3,500
Current liabilities	
Trade payables	1,786
Tax liabilities	925
	2,711
Total liabilities	6,211
Total equity and liabilities	33,161

Required:

Calculate relevant performance indicator ratios to one decimal place. Include ratios to cover profitability, liquidity and gearing.

3.4   A business may engage in 'window dressing' when producing a set of financial statements. The organisation may delay payments to suppliers and try to speed up credit control. This makes the cash position of the business look better than it normally is and distorts key performance indicators, such as trade receivables collection period and trade payables payment period.

This is an example of what?

(a)	Engaging in unethical behaviour	✓
(b)	Engaging in fraudulent behaviour	
(c)	Complying with loan terms	
(d)	Implementing accounting standards	

3.5   The password policy for a business is for all employees to change their password each month, but currently many employees do not do so. If the update is automatically required by the accounting system, what principle would this be supporting?

(a)	Objectivity	
(b)	Confidentiality	✓
(c)	Professional competence and due care	
(d)	Social equality	

3.6   You work as the Financial Accountant for a recruitment company. You have one member of staff in your accounts team who would like to study for her AAT but is currently unable to pay for it herself.

By paying for her training, what principle would you be supporting?

(a)	Environmental protection	
(b)	Objectivity	
(c)	Social equality	✓
(d)	Professional behaviour	

3.7 You have recently asked for suggestions from the employees in your company to improve ethical and sustainable practices where you work. The company is growing quickly, as sales volumes are doubling each year.

Identify which of the following would be a way to improve ethics and sustainability. Tick all options that apply.

(a)	Install solar panels on the factory roof	✓
(b)	Implement a flexible pricing strategy, charging much higher prices when products are temporarily in short supply	
(c)	Review level of overtime in finance department every quarter, to determine if more staff are required	✓

3.8 Your colleague has made the following statements about financial information produced by the finance department. Indicate whether the statements are correct or not correct.

		Type of financial information	Correct / Not correct
(a)	The statement of financial position is used to show the cash used to invest in assets in the business	Financial	Not correct
(b)	The budgetary control reports will be distributed to managers responsible for this part of the budget	Management	Correct

4 Internal control systems and fraud

this chapter covers...

The main part of this chapter explains the internal control systems that are set up in an organisation to implement all the requirements of external regulations and other organisational requirements.

The chapter covers the different types of fraud and how and when they may occur. How to prevent and detect fraud are considered, along with the impact of fraud on the businesses.

The chapter also describes in detail:

- *the purpose of internal control systems*

- *the types of internal controls used in different parts of the accounting system*

- *how the type of internal controls needed are influenced by the type of organisation*

- *the importance of strong internal controls systems to keep the risk of loss, through error or fraud, to a minimum*

- *how ethics and strong internal controls support each other*

- *the different types of fraud that can be committed within an organisation*

- *the risk of fraud occurring within an organisation*

- *the areas vulnerable to fraud*

- *the need to design a system so that fraud is minimised, can be easily detected and dealt with as appropriate*

- *the implications for an organisation if fraud occurs*

INTERNAL CONTROL IN AN ACCOUNTING SYSTEM

why do we need internal control systems?

Any accounting system will have certain elements in common, whether it is a company Accounts Department, a Local Authority Purchasing Department or a charitable organisation's fundraising section. It will:

- deal with money – handling cash

- need to make payments and sometimes issue cheques

- have 'levels of authority' within the system

- need to make decisions over ordering and purchasing

- need to set budgets for spending

- need to organise its accounting records

Unless management is happy to let everything become totally disorganised, the accounting system will need to establish various **rules and regulations** which will establish an **internal control system,** for example:

- the establishing of **money limits** for certain transactions

- the definition of **levels of responsibility** for **authorising** transactions

- the need for **referral of decision making** to another person when required

the importance of a strong internal control system

A strong internal control system gives managers confidence that:

- serious errors or missing items in the financial statements are unlikely

- the risk of fraud occurring is as low as possible

- the business can operate smoothly and efficiently

- the assets of the business are protected, or safeguarded

- any financial reports produced are of good quality – ie accurate and as up-to-date as possible, including all liabilities

- the business will comply with relevant regulations and legislation

This is summarised in the diagram on the next page:

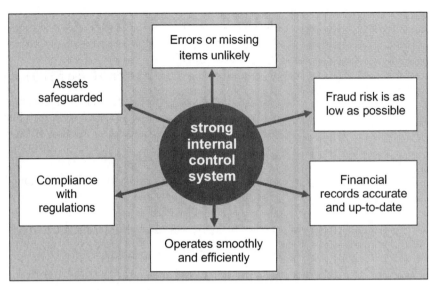

It is important to note that it is the responsibility of senior management to ensure there are strong internal control systems in place.

TYPES OF INTERNAL CONTROL SYSTEMS

large and medium-sized organisations

Often a medium-sized or large organisation will have policies and procedures in place, which form part of the internal control system.

Illustrated on the next page are extracts from a **Policies and Procedures** internal control document issued by the Accounts and Finance Department of a medium-sized business. Read through this and you will see that there are a number of examples of internal controls. These have been extracted and are shown below.

---

controls over money limits

All orders of £1,000 or more must be authorised by the budget holder.

All cheques for £1,000 or over require two signatories.

Petty cash will be topped up on the 'imprest' system, where the amount spent is reimbursed. It is intended for small items, up to £20.

controls over authorisation

All invoices must be authorised for payment by the budget holder.

Salary payments require the signature of the Accounts Manager or Financial Controller, plus one other.

referral to another person or higher authority (authorisation controls)

Budget holders will discuss with the Financial Controller appropriate parameters, plus maximum allowed deviations, before the budget holder or senior manager is brought in; this will be documented.

Finance must be informed if there are queries delaying authorisation (of payments) or if payment is to be withheld for any reason.

POLICIES AND PROCEDURES STATEMENT– ACCOUNTING AND FINANCE (extracts)

Books of account and records

Proper accounting records will be kept. The accounts systems is based around computer facilities, using Sage and Excel, but manual/paper records will also be used if appropriate. The following records will be kept:

- Appropriate control accounts (bank control, petty cash control, VAT control, salary control)

- Monthly trial balances

- Petty cash and bank accounts will be reconciled at least monthly

- VAT Returns produced on the required quarterly cycle

Ordering supplies and services

Budget holders can place orders for goods or services within their budget areas, subject only to cash-flow restraints. All orders of £1,000 or more must be authorised by the budget holder, except for specific areas of expenditure where written procedures have been agreed. Under £1,000, the budget holder may delegate all ordering as appropriate. Budget holders will discuss with the Financial Controller appropriate parameters, plus maximum allowed deviations, before the budget holder or senior manager is brought in, which will be documented.

Payment authorisation and Payables Ledger

All invoices must be authorised for payment by the budget holder, although the actual checking of details may be delegated. The authorising department is responsible for checking invoices for accuracy in terms of figures and conformity with the order placed, that the services or goods have been received, and following up any problems. Finance must be informed if there are queries delaying authorisation or if payment is to be withheld for any reason.

A Payables Ledger is operated by Finance. All incoming invoices are to be passed to Finance section as soon as they arrive. Invoices will be recorded in the Payables Ledger within two days, unless there are coding problems. They are then passed on to budget holders for authorisation. Once authorised as above, suppliers will be paid within the appropriate timescale.

Cheque writing and signing

Signatories will only be drawn from senior staff and directors, and any new signatory must be approved by the directors before the bank is notified. All cheques for £1,000 or over require two signatories. Cheque signatories should check that the expenditure has been authorised by the appropriate person before signing the cheque. Salary payments require the signature of the Accounts Manager or Financial Controller, plus one other. Cheques should be filled in completely (with payee, amount in words and figures, and date) before cheques are signed.

Handling of cash

Petty cash will be topped up on the 'imprest' system, where the amount spent is reimbursed. It is intended for small items, up to £20. Anything over this should be paid by cheque where possible. The imprest has a balance limit of £250. The petty cash balance will be reconciled when restoring the imprest balance, or monthly if this is more frequent. All cash collected from Finance will be signed for, and receipts will be issued for all cash returned.

As you can see, an internal control system is made up a variety of individual controls over different elements of the purchasing process. We will consider the specific type of controls a business could put in place in particular accounting systems in Chapter 6, when we consider what makes an effective accounting system.

small organisations

A smaller organisation may have different accounting control systems, where the emphasis is more on key individuals using authorisation and management review controls, rather than written policies and procedures.

For example, in a small owner-managed business, there may only be one or two members of accounts staff. The accounts will be produced by this small team who are aware of the trading performance of the business and are likely to identify fraud or errors as and when they arise.

The owner will also be aware of most of the business's transactions, as they are probably going to be significantly involved with buying and selling items. As the owner is likely to be the main signatory, they will probably review all the payments as they are made and ask about anything they do not know about or do not understand, so errors or fraud by the accounts staff are less likely to happen. Similarly, the owner may track the sales figures and compare this to the management accounts, produced periodically, and investigate the difference themselves. This review process is likely to identify any errors or items which are missing – a strong internal control system.

However, with this type of system, there is little **segregation** of duties (see page 67) and the owner needs to be particularly aware of this, and watch carefully for potential fraud.

types of internal controls

The internal control system relies on several different types of controls to operate in all areas of the accounting systems. When we go on to look at effective accounting systems in Chapter 6, we will review the controls we expect to see in systems such as payroll, sales and purchasing. For now, you can see on the following page the type of controls which are commonly found in accounting systems:

Type of Control	Example
Segregation	The Accounts Receivable Clerk, who enters invoices, cannot receive and record cash receipts
Organisation	Clear, defined roles for staff in appropriate departments, eg Finance, Production, Human Resources
Authorisation	Credit notes over £2,000 need to be authorised by the Finance Director
Physical	Petty cash tin kept in a locked drawer
Supervision	The Management Accountant supervises the Accounts Payable Clerk to ensure duties are carried out to the required standard
Personnel	Qualified, competent staff
Arithmetical and accounting	The wages control account is reconciled regularly
Management	Management accounts are produced and reviewed each month, with variances investigated

the impact of ethics

The directors of a company and senior management will determine the culture of the organisation, which affects the environment in which the accounting system operates. If the directors behave ethically, employees are more likely to do this as well. Conversely, if the directors behave unethically, staff may believe this is acceptable. This could result in more instances of fraud and error, by both the directors and staff.

For example, Volkswagen is known to have misstated results for CO_2 emissions tests on its cars, so customers were misinformed when they purchased them. This was done knowingly by employees and is estimated to have cost Volkswagen 6.8 billion Euros. Had strong internal control systems been in place and the ethical standards been clear, this may not have happened at all.

A company with strong internal control systems can ensure ethical standards are maintained, for example:

- clear communication of the ethical values of the business puts integrity at the heart of dealing with everyone

- competent, qualified staff who are committed to their work and ensure they perform it to a high standard will comply with professional competence and due care

- directors and managers who follow relevant rules and regulations behave professionally

- decisions being made using set authorisation limits will be carried out in an objective, unbiased manner

causes of weaknesses in the accounting system

In Chapter 6, we will look in detail at the specific controls we expect in each accounting system, such a payroll or sales.

You will need to appreciate that if an accounting system has weaknesses, it will be because the system of internal controls is deficient in one way or another. There are several reasons why this can happen:

- **lack of controls** in the system

- **poor implementation** of controls

- **lack of monitoring** of controls

- **lack of leadership**

Let's look at these in more detail below, considering why each might occur.

lack of controls

- poorly designed system, with few controls within it

- lack of qualified, experienced staff to design appropriate controls

- the business has grown from a small business, and with no changes to the accounting systems, and the owner is no longer able to control it sufficiently

poor implementation of controls

- staff have left the business and new staff have not been trained in the importance of the control procedures properly

- unqualified, incompetent staff may not realise the importance of having controls, so prepare information separately from the accounting system

- controls are not integrated into daily, weekly or monthly procedures, so are forgotten about

lack of monitoring

- staff are 'too busy' to undertake a review of controls, such as inventory counts, due to under-staffing

- senior staff are unaware of the importance of monitoring, not simply performing, controls, to ensure they operate properly

- senior management 'trust' the staff to do their job properly, so monitoring is considered unnecessary

lack of leadership

- the owners are too busy running the business to spend time focusing on whether systems are working properly

- the finance function is located separately to the rest of the business and management

Weaknesses in the internal controls will lead to various possible problems:

- **errors being made** because people do not know the correct way of doing things

- errors being made **and not being picked up** because the processes are not being checked properly

- **fraud being committed** because the internal control system is deficient and the opportunity for fraud is there for the taking

TYPES OF FRAUD

Fraud is an unfortunate fact of life within organisations. It sometimes hits the headlines, as, for example, when a merchant banker's personal assistant diverted over £1 million of her employer's funds into designer clothes, cars, speedboats, and general high living. This is obviously an extreme example which makes good material for the media, but the principle involved is the same as the employee who walks off with the employer's stationery or petty cash, or who sneaks out of work an hour early to watch a football match.

Fraud covers a variety of offences, so a general definition of fraud is:

the use of deception with the intention of obtaining an advantage, avoiding an obligation or causing loss to someone else or to an organisation

Fraud is a criminal activity, covered in the UK by a number of laws:

theft	dishonestly taking someone else's property (Theft Act)
false accounting	dishonestly destroying, defacing, concealing or falsifying an accounting record for personal gain or to cause loss to someone else (Theft Act)
bribery and corruption	taking or giving a bribe that might influence the actions of others (The Bribery Act)
deception	obtaining property, money, services or evading liability by deception (Theft Act)

It should be noted that there are two types of fraud – financial and non-financial.

financial fraud

Financial fraud within an organisation can often be described as an activity which presents a risk of some form of loss to the employer:

- **loss of money**, eg theft of petty cash

- **loss of inventory**, eg theft of products by supermarket staff

- **loss of time**, eg disappearing from work to do something else during contracted work hours

All of these frauds are a **misappropriation of funds** from the business, either directly or indirectly.

Fraud can also occur when there is a **misstatement of the financial statements**:

- **one-off (singular) misstatement**, eg not recording lease liabilities in the financial statements to keep the gearing of the business low, in order to secure additional loans

- **continuing misstatement over time**, eg increasing the value of closing inventory over a period of several years to show consistent growth in profits. This could keep attracting new investors

non-financial fraud

Let's think back to the Volkswagon fraud. The employees did not receive money to amend the test results but knowingly deceived the regulators. The people who purchased the non-compliant cars 'lost out' on owning a low emission car and may also have had higher tax bills if it was a company car.

management's responsibility regarding fraud

It is the responsibility of the management of an organisation to:

- identify areas where the **risk of fraud** exists and to grade the seriousness of the risk in each case

- set up **control systems** involving all staff to alert management to the possible occurrence of fraud

- monitor those control systems on a regular basis to ensure that they are working

- deal with any incidence of fraud in an appropriate way, whether it be a formal warning or calling in the police

practical examples of fraud

In practical terms fraud is normally a combination of any of the following:

- theft of property or money or information (eg someone copying and selling the company's customer database to a competitor)

- falsification of records so that property or money is passed to the wrong person (eg fictitious employee set up on the payroll)

- collusion – ie a 'set-up' between an employee and someone else outside the organisation (eg false invoices sent in by an outsider for supplies that were never made, and authorised and paid by the person 'on the inside')

public examples of fraud

There are many examples of fraud which are made public. The examples below have been adapted from cases reported by a leading insurance company.

REPORTED CASES OF FRAUD

Theft of fuel inventories – Total Loss £25,000

A local authority had their own fuel pumps for supplying their motor vehicles. The employee in charge stole fuel over a long period as the inventory checks were inadequate.

Payroll fraud: fictitious employees – Total Loss £10,000

The manager of an industrial cleaning company invented bogus employees, put them on the payroll and then cashed their pay cheques.

Bank deposits: teeming and lading – in 10 months a total of £7,000 was stolen

A clerk in charge of a sub post office stole cash receipts due to be paid into the local bank. This was covered up by delaying paying in at the bank and altering the paying-in slips relating to subsequent deposits. Stealing money received from one source and then using money received from other sources to cover it up is known as 'teeming and lading'.

Cheque printing machine – Total Loss £25,000

A Ledger Clerk responsible for making regular payment of rent for advertising was in charge of a machine that printed cheques. Numerous small cheques were made out by him for the correct amounts but payable to him. It was several months before complaints from suppliers (who had not received their cheques) were investigated and the fraud uncovered.

Collusion: inventories control system – Total Loss £1 million

A well known national company was defrauded by two gangs of employees working at the same location. The losses involved collusion between warehouse staff and drivers who used the spare capacity on vehicles to remove goods from the depot. False information was entered into the computerised inventory control system and their activities were only discovered when the police reported finding large amounts of the particular product in the hands of third parties.

Collusion: fictitious sub-contractors – Total Loss exceeded £500,000

A major contractor with well established control systems to approve payments were the victims of fraud by a section supervisor in collusion with a computer operator. Cheques were made out to fictitious sub-contractors and despatched to private addresses.

RISK ASSESSMENT AND FRAUD

risk assessment – the role of management

Assessment of **fraud risk** is part of the **risk assessment** process which is the responsibility of organisations in both the private and the public sectors.

In the case of limited companies (private sector), the Turnbull Report has stated that directors have responsibility for ensuring that risk management practices are established as part of an effective internal control system.

In the public sector, the International Public Sector Fraud Forum produced a document regarding fraud risk 'A Guide to Managing Fraud for Public Bodies', which is available as a download from https://assets.publishing.service.gov.uk.

The assessment of risk generally by management follows a number of distinct stages. This process applies equally to the assessment of fraud risk:

- setting up a risk management group and identifying objectives

- identifying the areas at risk of fraud

- grading the scale of the risk in each case

- developing a strategy to manage or mitigate that risk by taking appropriate action

- setting up systems to ensure compliance with legal and regulatory obligations

- monitoring the running of the system

- reviewing and reporting on the system to determine if the risk is being managed

Once we have looked at effective accounting systems in Chapter 6, we will consider how to monitor, review and report on if the potential risks in the system are being managed, including fraud risk.

the internal control system – fraud prevention

A robust internal control system is essential if management is going to be able to detect and deal with fraud.

There are various techniques that can be used for making an internal control system 'fraud resistant':

- **fraud staff**

  Some very large organisations may appoint employees – eg ex-bank or ex-police staff – to work full-time on fraud prevention and detection.

- **management responsibility**

  Managers should be given specific areas of responsibility and answerability – eg sections of the Accounts Department – to ensure that fraud is kept to a minimum.

- **management supervision**

  Management – particularly line management – should supervise accounting activities on a regular basis. This involves overseeing and checking activities such as data entry to computers, making payments and payroll processing.

- **segregation of duties**

  The system should be set up so that duties which, when combined, could lead to fraud, are given to different people – ie they are segregated. For example, the cashier taking in cash for a business should ideally not be the same person who makes out the paying-in slip for the bank. The danger is that some of the cash may disappear into the cashier's pocket.

- **lock and key**

  Physical security – locking valuable items away – is a sure deterrent to theft. This does not only apply to cash: the tendency of items such as laptop computers and mobile phones to disappear has become a well-known and ever-increasing statistic.

- **authorisation**

  Some accounting activities may require authorisation by a nominated official. This ranges from the authorisation of petty cash and signing of cheques over a certain amount, to the investing of liquid funds, eg placing £250,000 on a money market account. Clearly the larger the amount, the more senior the person giving authorisation.

detecting fraud

We have already seen the various areas in which fraud can occur. Fraud can be detected by the experienced manager by simple observation and through experience. Some of the tell-tale and danger signs include:

- employees acting suspiciously – looking worried and hiding paperwork

- employees with higher levels of spending than you would expect from their income – the Payroll Clerk who has a new Porsche

- employees working long hours and taking less than the normal holiday entitlement – it is often when employees are away that other employees notice suspicious signs and uncover criminal activity

- employees who have a grudge against the organisation – they may have been passed over for promotion or they may even have a political or ethical axe to grind

■ employees who are known to be short of money – they may be struggling with a high mortgage or may even have a drugs problem

grading likelihood and impact

Part of the process of the management of fraud risk is the decision about whether a risk is a **likely** one or not. The likelihood of risk can be divided into three levels:

■ **high** – the likelihood of fraud is at a high level (disappearing biros)

■ **medium** – the likelihood is possible (theft of cash, collusion)

■ **low** – the likelihood is remote (removal of assets from a company pension fund)

The risk of fraud occurring can also be given a **numerical value**: for example, a range of 1 to 5, where the higher the risk the higher the number.

Risk assessment also needs to decide whether the **impact** of the fraud is significant. Impact can relate to the **financial state** of the organisation. A major loss through fraud could seriously affect profit and liquidity. For example, the fraudulent trading by an employee of Barings Bank led to its collapse. The fraud can also seriously affect employees, as in the Robert Maxwell case in which employees' pensions were appropriated by the Chairman and Chief Executive.

Generally speaking, frauds that are likely (the disappearing biro) have a lower impact than the remote risk (removal of assets from a company pension fund). The **impact** of a fraud can therefore be similarly graded:

■ **high** – the effects of fraud are very serious for the organisation, affecting its profit and/or liquidity

■ **medium** – the effects of the fraud are significant but can be dealt with internally, or in some cases by the police (theft, collusion)

■ **low** – the impact of the fraud is insignificant (petty pilfering)

using a matrix to grade fraud risk

Organisations sometimes use a matrix to assess the extent of fraud risk in an accounting system. The areas of the system in which the fraud might occur must first be identified, for example:

■ cash payments

■ cash receipts

■ receivables ledger

■ payables ledger

■ expenses

■ inventory control

- payroll
- non-current asset purchase

A matrix (or a section of a matrix) will then be drawn up for each of the areas identified. An example of entries in a typical matrix is illustrated below. The matrix might display:

- the identified risk area of the organisation
- the details of the type of fraud
- the role of the employee who may become involved in it
- any third party who may become involved through collusion
- the likelihood of the fraud (high, moderate, low)
- the impact of the fraud (high, moderate, low)
- the suggested control to prevent the fraud

This matrix will then become a valuable tool which will enable management to assess the risks and establish an appropriate strategy for minimising them. Note that the format of the matrices you will encounter in your studies may vary. The example below is fairly typical.

accounting system fraud risk matrix – some sample entries

Details of Risk	Employees	Collusion	Likelihood	Impact	Suggested control
Payroll section: Stationery pilferage	payroll staff	none	high	low	Lock cabinet. One person controls access
Theft of cash	payroll staff	none	medium	medium	Two people assemble cash pay packets
Payments to fictitious employees	payroll staff	third party recipients	medium	medium	Review of payroll. BACS authorisation by Finance Director and one other
Payables ledger: Paying fictitious suppliers etc . . . etc . . .	buyer	third party recipients	medium	medium	Only Purchasing Manager can access supplier master files to set up new suppliers and their bank details

Answering the assessment

As part of the assessment, you may be asked to identify potential frauds, evaluate the likelihood of fraud, the impact for the business and consider what you do to prevent it from happening in the future. As you become more familiar with effective systems and the controls you expect to see in accounting systems (Chapter 6), you can then see when controls are missing and hence where the opportunity for fraud may exist.

THE IMPACT OF FRAUD

financial impact

When fraud occurs, a business may suffer financial loss. How significant the financial impact is often depends on how large the fraud is.

For example, a person stealing from petty cash each week will be committing a serious but low value fraud, which is unlikely to cause the business significant harm in the long-term. However, the employees who misreported the data for Volkswagen, and committed the fraud, have already had a significant financial impact on the business. The company has provided €6.8 billion to cover expected costs relating to the fraud, which is equal to the entire operating profit for 2014. Volkswagen has the reserves to deal with such a large claim. However, a business with less financial strength could cease to operate if the financial loss is very significant.

non-financial impact

The financial impact of a fraud can often be measured reliably. However, the non-financial impact can be just as great but be harder to quantify. There may be damage to employee relations or reputation in the industry.

Volkswagen, for example, has misled customers, who may now no longer believe they can trust the business. This may stop them buying Volkswagen cars in the future and this lack of future sales will be very hard to measure. Current employees may feel that they no longer wish to work for Volkswagen and leave. Potential employees who could add value to Volkswagen's business may decide to work for another car company in preference. The damage to Volkswagen's reputation is impossible to measure and may affect their business for years ahead.

As you will have gathered from this chapter, fraud is inevitable. The lesson for the organisation is – be prepared.

This chapter concludes with two Case Studies on fraud and analysis of fraud published by HM Treasury. They should provide you with an understanding of how a weakness in the accounting system can make fraud possible.

Case Study

TRAVEL AND SUBSISTENCE FRAUD

situation

This fraud involved an employee who travelled regularly on official business. He set his own programme of visits which was not checked by his manager. He then regularly submitted fraudulent travel and subsistence claims which included examples of:

- Claiming subsistence allowances in excess of entitlement.

- Claiming for overnight stays in hotels when in fact he had stayed with friends or family.

- Claiming for visits not made.

- Forging authorising signatures.

- Inflating claims by altering details on claim forms after authorisation by countersigning officer.

These claims were paid by the finance team despite the lack of receipts, invoices or other supporting documents to verify his expenditure. Travel and subsistence guidance was also out-of-date and consequently had fallen into disuse.

The fraud came to light when his office tried to contact him at a hotel where he claimed to be staying. An investigation uncovered a large number of fraudulent claims spanning several years and the employee was eventually prosecuted.

required

Identify the weaknesses in the expenses system which allowed the fraud to take place.

solution

- Inadequate guidance on submitting, authorising and paying claims.

- Inadequate supervision by line management.

- Failure of countersigning officer to verify that journeys had been made.

- Inadequate control exercised by countersigning officer in returning signed claim forms to the claimant rather than passing them directly to the finance team.

- Inadequate checks by finance teams to query amendments to claims, verify countersignatures and ensure that receipts and invoices were included to substantiate claims.

- Absence of spot-checks on claims by the finance team management.

CASH HANDLING FRAUD

situation

Transactions involving receipts of cash or cheques are high risks. Of the cases of staff fraud reported to the Treasury each year, a significant proportion involves misappropriation of cash. In this Case Study, a member of staff committed a number of frauds over a period of five years, resulting in a loss of over £10,000.

The organisation's business included the receipt of cheques through the post and cash cheques over the counter. It was the responsibility of the member of staff to receive, record and prepare the receipts for banking. She had been in the job for several years and her line managers, who trusted her implicitly, had given her sole responsibility for these duties. They were no longer carrying out checks or monitoring the process.

She would arrive early each morning, usually before her colleagues, and open the post on her own. Money handed in over the counters was also passed to her for banking. However, she did not record or account for the cheques or money prior to banking. She would complete a daily cash balance record as part of the banking reconciliation procedures, but by this time she had already removed some of the cash and a number of cheques. There were no independent cross-checks between the documentation which came with the receipts and the amounts sent for banking. To make matters worse, written procedures were out-of-date and were unused.

The fraud came to light during the employee's infrequent holiday. A minor query by a member of the public regarding a previous payment led to an unexplained difference between the amount quoted in the documentation accompanying the payment and the amount recorded by the employee and banked.

Internal audit were brought in to carry out an initial investigation. They identified major discrepancies between records of receipts kept by counter staff, documentation accompanying payments from members of the public and the amounts being banked. The police were called in and under questioning the officer admitted the offences. She had opened a bank account with the initials of the organisation and had been paying in cash and cheques over a five year period. The case was taken to court and on conviction she was given a custodial sentence and had to repay the amount stolen.

required

Identify two types of fraud and the circumstances that may allow each type of fraud to take place.

solution

Type of fraud

Misappropriation of assets - money

Circumstances that may allow the fraud

- Theft of cheques and cash due to a lack of segregation of duties between post opening, preparation of cash and cheques for banking and reconciliation of amounts banked.
- Theft of cheques and cash due to inadequate supervision and monitoring by line management.

Type of fraud

Misstatement of financial statements – false accounting

Circumstances that may allow the fraud

- Incorrect recording of cash receipts due to absence of management checks of accounting records, cash balances or bank reconciliations.
- Incorrect recording of cash receipts due to lack of adequate written instructions and over-reliance on the honesty and integrity of one individual.
- Incorrect recording of cash receipts due to unawareness of implications of reluctance to use holiday entitlement.

Note: The internal audit report also identified organisational factors which had contributed to the fraud. The main ones were:

- the organisation had not assessed the risk of fraud
- there was no policy statement on fraud
- line managers were not clear about their responsibilities
- manuals and procedures were poorly structured and out-of-date

Chapter Summary

- Businesses need internal control systems to protect their assets, ensure liabilities are recorded, minimise fraud and error and ensure data is accurate and up-to-date.

- Internal controls are individual activities that form part of the internal control system, such as authorisation and qualified personnel.

- Large organisations may have policies and procedures written down for staff to comply with, as part of their internal control system.

- Small organisations will rely on senior management review and authorisation by owners/directors to minimise fraud and error in the business.

- A strong internal controls system can support strong ethical values in an organisation.

- Types of fraud include misappropriation of assets (theft), misstatement of financial statements (false accounting or reporting), bribery and deception. Sometimes fraud involves collusion, where two people work together to commit fraud.

- The directors of the business are required to protect the business against fraud and error. They must put controls in place to do this.

- A business may review its policies and procedures to identify the areas where fraud is most likely and to consider the impact of fraud on it. They may grade the likelihood, either using High, Medium or Low or a grading system 1 to 5, where the higher the number the greater the risk.

- The impact of fraud can be financial, in the form of lost income or assets. There can also be non-financial impacts, such as loss of reputation and custom in the future. Employees may leave or refuse to join such a business.

Key Terms		
	internal control	a process put in place by management to prevent or detect fraud or errors eg authorisation, segregation
	internal control system	the rules and regulations, including internal controls, in place in an accounting system eg payroll to detect and prevent fraud and error
	segregation of duties	the separation of the responsibility for the recording of a financial transaction (eg a sale) and the responsibility for the recording of its settlement (ie the customer paying)
	policies and procedures	internal documents issued by the Finance Department stating how accounting items should be dealt with by the business eg purchases and payments, sales and credit control
	fraud	the use of deception with the intention of obtaining an advantage, avoiding an obligation or causing loss to someone else or to an organisation
	fraud grading assessment	the process where a potential fraud is given a grade – High, Medium or Low or 1 to 5 (5 being the most likely) – of it occurring

Activities

4.1   For each of the weaknesses given below, indicate the cause.

Select causes of weaknesses from:

Lack of leadership, lack of controls, lack of monitoring and poor implementation of controls
1   2   3   4

(a)	Authorisation limits for purchases are not in place	2
(b)	Losses or gain on the inventory count are not investigated and are simply written off to profit or loss	4
(c)	Bank reconciliations are performed every three or four months	3
(d)	Management are often absent as they travel to see customers or suppliers	1

4.2   For each of the controls below, identify whether the internal control is suitable for the purpose given.

Internal control	Purpose	Control suitable - Yes or No?
The Financial Accountant reviews the BACS payment for wages and compares it to payroll, prior to authorising it along with the Financial Director	Prevent and detect fraud	Yes
Two people open the post each day to record customer receipts	Compliance	No
Monthly backups of data to an offsite server	Safeguard assets	No

4.3 Caraben's Costume Hire Ltd is based in Oxford and is run by Cara and her brother Ben. It supplies theatres and TV production companies across the UK with period costumes. It offers regular customers 30 days credit and will accept cash, with a returnable deposit, from new businesses. It employs 10 staff, who have been with the company for several years.

Cash sales are recorded through the till, with each deposit being kept in an envelope with the customer's name on, in an old petty cash tin, ready from when the costumes are returned. Cash takings are banked weekly.

Cara phones credit customers once a month to ask them to pay, which they generally do.

Complete the following statement:

The above may result in the occurrence of [~~inventory~~ / **theft of cash** / ~~profit manipulation~~] fraud that occurs as a result of [~~poor implementation of controls / lack of leadership~~ / **lack of controls**]. In order to address this fraud risk, Cara and Ben need to implement [**a series of physical controls** / ~~reconciliation controls / authorisation controls~~] as soon as possible, to minimise the impact on the [**assets** / ~~liabilities~~].

4.4 You have recently moved from the finance department of a large company to a small one, to improve the internal control systems. As part of this process, your employer has asked you to identify which internal controls will be most suitable for her business.

Identify which of the following controls are more suitable for either a large or small business. Tick the correct column.

Internal control	Small	Large
Segregation of duties for the posting of sales invoices and credit notes, receiving customer receipts and updating the trade receivables ledger		✓
All payments are authorised by the Managing Director	✓	
Daily bank reconciliations are performed, using automated software		✓

4.5 Design For life is keen to develop a reputation for ethical behaviour. A review of the finance department identified that some of the systems did not currently promote ethical behaviours. You have been given several suggestions to address this.

Identify which of the following would promote ethical behaviours within Design For Life Ltd.

Improvement	Promote	Not promote
Ensure originals of qualifications for new employees are obtained and copied	✓	
The accounting system requires automatic password changes every 30 days for all staff	✓	
A register of employees who have relationships with staff at customers or suppliers is maintained and regularly reviewed	✓	
A new policy allows finance staff to work from home for up to five days per month, to save them commuter time and travel costs		✓

4.6 Who is responsible for ensuring the accounting systems and controls are designed to prevent and detect fraud? Tick the appropriate option below.

(a)	The Finance Director	
(b)	The Managing Director	
(c)	The Human Resources Director	
(d)	All of the above	✓

4.7 List the common types of fraud.

4.8 Explain what segregation of duties is and how it prevents fraud, giving an example.

4.9 Gino Giardino runs Giardino Services Ltd, a successful gardening business, providing garden maintenance services to customers, both business premises and private households. He employs five people and provides them each with garden equipment and a small van. Their main job involves cutting and maintaining lawns and hedging on a fixed contract with each customer. The same people look after the same customers each month. Each gardener completes a weekly timesheet stating how long they have spent at each customer's house or premises. Gino pays them a fixed hourly rate, based on this timesheet.

Periodically, customers will request one-off jobs to be done, such as pruning and weeding whilst the gardener is there. These are done on a cash basis and each employee is given an invoice book, in which to record the sale. They put the cash in their cash tin and return the tin and invoice book to Gino once a week. He banks the receipts and uses his bank statement to update sales.

Required:

(a) Identify and explain two possible frauds which could occur.

(b) Grade the risk on the business of each fraud, using the grading system High, Moderate or Low.

(c) Identify the potential implications of each risk identified.

(d) For each fraud, identify one safeguard Gino could put in place to reduce the risk of the fraud happening.

4.10 Lift Express Limited undertook a review of its activities recently and identified the following potential frauds. There are no controls currently in place to prevent them. Complete the grading table and a possible control to prevent and/or detect the possible fraud.

Details of possible fraud	Employees	Collusion	Likelihood*	Possible control
IT Theft of customer pricing due to open access to files	Accounts, IT	None	*High*	
Payroll Wages payments overstated on timesheets	Production hourly paid	None	*High*	
Warehouse Taking inventory for own use or selling on	Stores, Production	Third party recipients	*Medium*	

*Grade either high, medium or low

5 Technology and accounting systems

this chapter covers...

The main part of this chapter explains how technological changes may affect accounting systems.

The chapter covers the different types of technology that may be used within accounting systems and how technology impacts on financial reporting.

The chapter describes in detail:

- *the impact of cloud accounting on accounting systems*

- *how artificial intelligence may affect accounting systems*

- *the different types of data analytics and how using it can affect accounting systems*

- *the need for data security*

- *the risks to data and operations arising from the use of technology*

- *how accounting software presents information to non-financial managers*

- *how 'visualisation' improves the financial understanding of managers and clients*

TECHNOLOGY AND THE ACCOUNTING SYSTEM

why is technology important?

Advances in technology are changing the way we work all the time. The ability to hold meetings 'virtually' reduces the need for employees to travel and improves staff productivity. 'Smart' tills can not only record sales, but also hold and monitor inventory levels, raise orders to replenish inventory and report on the gross profit margin by product for thousands of items.

The finance function is no exception to experiencing changing technology and successful accountants must embrace and understand relevant technologies to provide the best possible service to both the business and its clients.

Let's look at recent technological changes and how they may affect accounting systems.

CLOUD ACCOUNTING

A **cloud accounting** system allows users to access information and enter data via the internet. A business-based system stored data on a server based in the building, accessed via a local network, using desktop or laptop computers. Cloud accounting systems have become increasingly popular in recent years for several reasons.

features of cloud accounting

Cloud accounting software works the same as any other type of accounting software but there are two key differences:

- **data is stored remotely** – data is not held in the business and the accounting system is automatically updated as each piece of data is added

- **multiple user access** – several employees can access data and files from different locations and see the same data

Typically, the business pays for cloud accounting on a monthly or annual basis, based on the number of users.

benefits of cloud accounting

Let's consider the benefits of cloud accounting, over a business-based accounting system.

- **remote access**

Employees can access data from anywhere, as long as there is a stable internet connection. If employees are unable to travel, this means they can work at home, saving travelling time and money.

This also benefits large organisations, who operate in several locations across the world, as all companies can access data and information as if they were in the same place.

■ **shared access**

Finance often needs to share reports with different parts of the business. In a business-based system, large reports might be emailed, slowing down the system, or put onto a USB stick, which may be lost or stolen. Cloud accounting allows all parts of the organisation to see the same information at the same time, enabling the production director to access the standard costing variances for a particular product, without needing to wait for it to be sent to them by finance.

■ **improved sustainability**

Using cloud accounting reduces an organisation's use of paper, as many systems can send invoices and statements of account to customers electronically.

■ **lower IT costs**

As the business does not have to buy its own server, this hardware cost is avoided. The need for an IT department is reduced and no back-up processes are required, so the risk of losing data is lower and the overall IT costs are lower.

■ **better security**

Many cloud accounting software companies will use a data centre, with sophisticated levels of security to protect both the software and the data. There is no need to back up the data periodically, as this is automatic. This is particularly beneficial to smaller businesses.

Another benefit is that the data is not stored on the laptop, so if it is left on a train by an employee, or stolen, if the appropriate passwords are in place, the data will be safe.

risks of using cloud accounting

Choosing to use a cloud accounting is not without risk, as set out below:

■ **control and security of data**

Even with appropriate security in place, the business is putting sensitive and confidential data in the hands of a third party, via the internet, increasing the risk of unauthorised access of this data.

■ **reliance on internet access**

When 'the wifi doesn't work', neither do the finance staff! A strong internet connection is essential, otherwise month-end reporting with be late and the day-to-day operations will be disrupted.

INTELLIGENT ACCOUNTING SOFTWARE

Storing data is becoming cheaper, so the volume of it a business collects is increasing. Often, a business wants to use the data it collects regarding customers, sales, production costs, inventory levels, etc to aid decision making and add value to their business, ultimately increasing profitability.

High volumes of data will be processed and analysed using software that is 'clever', learning where to record and store data as it comes into the organisation.

In the finance department, many of the day-today tasks are repetitive, such as posting invoices to the payables ledger or reconciling the bank, so using accounting software that is 'clever' would improve efficiency and make reporting more accurate.

Artificial intelligence (AI) is the concept of creating a machine that can simulate the way humans think and behave. **Machine learning** is an application of AI that allows computers to learn from data, without being programmed explicitly. A social media company will target account holders with specific advertising, based on their previous purchasing history – it has 'learnt' what the person likes to buy. Similarly, media streaming services, such as Netflix, suggest shows you may like to watch, based on your previous viewing.

AI, machine learning and the finance function

So how does AI and machine learning apply to an accounting system? A simple example is when a purchase invoice is received for an *existing* inventory item and supplier and it is scanned into the system, the accounting system *'knows'* the transaction, so automatically updates the appropriate inventory record and updates the correct supplier account in the payables ledger.

The applications for machine learning are numerous, for example:

- **coding of data** – automatic coding of invoices, receipts and purchases should lead to accurate and prompt reporting

- **audit of information** – large amounts of data can be reviewed and any 'unexpected' items in an account highlighted, for further investigation

- **predictive models can be used to forecast data** – this is particularly useful for data analytics (see next section)

- **analysing multi-dimensional or multi-variety data** – this can be useful where the data is too complex for individual finance staff to analyse

the impact of AI on the finance function

implementation and cost

Creating and implementing bespoke machine learning is costly, due to the complexity of the programming and lack of programmers able to work with such complex programming. There are also ongoing running costs, as information changes and the format in which the data is received may also change over time, so the programming will need amending. This means machine learning software is only created by larger companies, who can afford to do it. Smaller companies may decide to purchase an 'off the shelf' cloud accounting system that has built in machine learning.

As the 'clever' accounting system 'does the work' it is sometimes hard for finance staff to accept the results in the reports that are produced – it is harder to 'trust' the information as they do not understand exactly how it has been processed.

Finally, some finance staff may be made redundant, as their work will be performed by the AI accounting system. This can make staff very resistant to this type of system being implemented, which the company must carefully consider.

However, it should be noted that the reporting and information produced still needs to be rigorously reviewed – such a system is not able to learn as well as a person ...and it will make mistakes!

DATA ANALYTICS

types of data analytics

Data analytics is another set of software tools that can be used in the finance function. It is the process of examining data in order to draw conclusions about the information within it. The four types of analytics are:

- **descriptive** – what has happened in the business?

- **diagnostic** – why did it happen?

- **predictive** – what is likely to happen next?

- **prescriptive** – what action do we need to take now?

Let's look at some practical examples of how each type of data analytic might relate to the work carried out by the finance function, to help us understand each type.

descriptive

- accurately recording high volumes of revenue and cost information

- reporting on weekly or monthly sales

- producing the actual figures for a set of monthly management accounts, along with the variances against budget

This type of data analytics looks at the actual data, reporting on past performance, with no further explanation.

diagnostic

- producing more detailed information on why variances occurred eg drilling down into sales and margin by product and/or location

- reviewing trends of material prices and finding out if there are exceptions to them and why that might be

The financial reporting team will usually do detailed analysis, enabling the business to learn from its mistakes, as well as spot possible opportunities to be exploited.

predictive

- looking at trends to determine the likelihood of the sales forecast for the next quarter

- identifying which costs are likely to increase, based on the data used in diagnostic analytics, to determine future cost forecasts

This use of data analytics is critical for large companies to build robust forecasts, using high volumes of data to produce them. It is important to remember, however, that predictive analytics needs accurate, high quality data and that forecasting is ever only an 'educated guess'!

prescriptive

- using internal and external information to assess the potential for a new product

- identifying when a product should be discontinued, due to changes in sales or cost levels

This might use machine learning, algorithms (complex mathematical tools) and rules set by the business together to create the resulting predictions and recommendations. This type of analytics is good for problem solving.

the impact of data analytics on the accounting system

Handling large volumes of data quickly and efficiently enables automated reporting, particularly for large companies. Using data analytics can speed up the reporting processes in finance, enabling decision making to be quicker.

Data analytics may also reduce the risk of fraud. For example, if the cash sales in a branch of a large multi-site retail business were consistently lower when a particular staff member was on site, diagnostic analytics could easily pick this up, by comparing cash sales data of this branch with other branches and interrogating the payroll system.

Data analytics can also help to identify opportunities in the business to work smarter, not simply harder. A retail business that spends a lot of time managing its distribution network might use data analytics to determine whether outsourcing this to a specialist company would be beneficial.

It could also be used to focus the business on particular activities and prioritise the most profitable. Using predictive and prescriptive data analytics can allow management to model whether to focus on improving production or product development to increase profitability.

It is worth noting that using predictive and prescriptive data analytics can be expensive, particularly if algorithms need to be written to undertake the analysis, so a business needs to consider the cost-benefit of implementing their use.

The use of data analytics can also be a cause for ethical concerns. Writing an algorithm, or mathematical programme, relies on certain assumptions being made – for example, historic patterns are an appropriate basis for future predictions. In 2020 in the UK, algorithms were used to predict an individual's exam result, based on national and local historic school data, rather than that individual's performance. Ethical concerns were raised when the results were released, as the algorithms were considered to be biased and unfair.

PROTECTING THE BUSINESS'S DATA

data security

When a business uses and stores information on computers, both on companies and on individuals, it must use **data security** to protect this information and to prevent unauthorised access. There are several reasons for this:

- compliance with data protection laws (such as the Data Protection Act 2018, which implements the General Data Protection Regulation, known as GDPR) to avoid heavy fines
- to enable the business to operate effectively, so the information is available when needed
- to keep information confidential, in payroll, for example
- to maintain the integrity of the information, so reports produced from it are accurate and valid

maintaining security

To protect the data and information, a business will use access controls, such as passwords, to give only authorised employees access to, say, the general ledger or the payroll system. In the accounting system this is particularly important as it supports a strong internal control system, so purchases are authorised appropriately and segregation of duties is maintained.

There will also be system-wide security controls, such as company firewalls, that protect against outside access.

risks to data and operations

In Chapter 4, we discussed fraud as a 'fact of life' and increasingly criminals are targeting IT systems. There have also been stories in the press of government laptops containing confidential information being left on trains, compromising national security, which was very embarrassing for the UK Government at the time.

Let's look at the following risks to data and operations businesses face, due to the technology we use today.

■ **cyberattacks**

A **cyberattack** is an attempt by hackers to gain access to, damage or destroy a computer network or system. There are several different types of cyberattack criminals may use. A common method is 'phishing', when an email is sent, pretending to be from a reputable company, asking for information such as passwords and credit card numbers or to update details of bank accounts, by clicking through to another site. It is often hard to tell if the email is real or not, particularly when it is from an address similar to one known to you, such as the bank or a supplier. Once the information is given, the criminal can use it to steal money from the business.

Malicious software, known as '**malware**' is another type of cyberattack. These are viruses that can be hidden in an attachment to an email, designed to disrupt, damage or gain unauthorised entry to a computer system. The business could suffer financial loss, through access to bank details, or be unable to access files or carry out day-to-day operations because of it. Installing anti-virus software helps manage this risk but sometimes this can slow down the speed the computer runs at as it is constantly checking the data flowing in and out of it. It is important staff are aware of the reasons for anti-virus software and do not disable it!

When a **ransomware** programme enters the accounting system, it locks the users out and will only allow them back in once the criminal is paid, often in cryptocurrency. Criminals target older versions of operating systems, such as Microsoft Windows, where it is easier to access the system. In May 2017, the National Health Service was subject to a ransomware attack, causing thousands of hospital appointments and treatments to be cancelled and delays to operations, as no-one could access patients' records. It is estimated to have cost the National Health Service £92million (*The Guardian, 12 January 2020, Jonathan Chan*).

■ **unauthorised access**

A computer could be accessed, either remotely or in the business, by someone who is not authorised. A hacker might try to access sensitive or confidential information to sell on the 'dark web', or it could be a disgruntled employee who wants to sell pricing information to a competitor. Whatever the reason, the result is likely to have serious consequences for the businesses and its future profitability. To avoid it, good access security, not sharing or writing down passwords, and a strong firewall are all required.

■ **loss of computer equipment**

As we mentioned earlier, sometimes laptops or tablets can be left on trains or in cars, and are lost or stolen. The data stored on them can be valuable to the right person. If the computer has not been backed-up properly recently, reports may need to be re-written and records recreated, wasting valuable resources in the business. Having clear policies regarding looking after company equipment and making staff personally responsible for items they use will help manage this risk.

■ **data issued in error**

Sometimes, when we are in a hurry, we might accidentally dial the wrong number or choose the wrong person to message from our telephone contacts. This can happen at work as well, when an employee accidentally sends an email to one customer who has a similar email address to another. It is an easy mistake to make, but this error could break the Data Protection Act 2018 and damage the relationship with either customer, particularly if it contained sensitive pricing or discount information, for example.

REPORTING FINANCIAL INFORMATION

Presenting complex financial information clearly and making it simple for non-financial managers to understand is important in the finance function. Some accounting software has reporting features built in it and can present the data using graphs and illustrations. The picture on the next page shows an example of the reporting for one such accounting software.

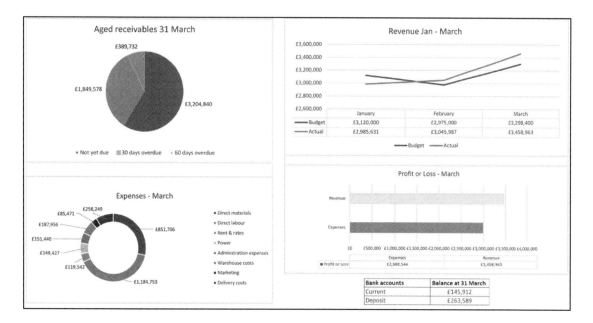

A small business may be able to easily keep control of revenue and expenses using these features as, even with no financial training, the business owner can see the critical issues to focus on.

Often accountants providing accounting services to clients will use a cloud accounting system with these features. The 'day-to-day' transactions are entered into the system by the client; then the accountant will review it, ensuring items are recorded in the right place, so that reports generated and used to manage the business are correct.

visualisation

In larger organisations, finance departments provide key performance indicators, forecasts and other critical information to help make decisions and enhance the company's performance. The volume of information in these organisations can be over-whelming and complex for non-financial managers, so **visualisation**, along with data analytics, can help. Visualisation is a method of showing the data visually that brings out its meaning. Studies have shown that 90% of the information entering the brain is visual, with colour increasing understanding and retention, so a picture really does paint a thousand words!

The graphs produced by the accounting system shown above are an example of 'visualisation' and are in a '**dashboard**' format. The five items set out key relevant information for the manager or client, using bar charts for invoicing information or a doughnut chart for expenses.

Different types of graph can also aid understanding, particularly if the volume of data is large. Presenting the data so it is not overwhelming and is easy for managers, or indeed clients, to interpret will enhance the company's financial understanding and aid decision making.

This sunburst chart below shows the proportion of revenue earned from travel shops based in Leeds, Bristol and London branches, along with the type of products sold in each place. This graph can be much easier for a non-financial manager to read and understand than a set of numbers on a sales report.

We often forget that the layout of financial information for accounts purposes can be quite confusing to non-financial managers. To ensure the information being used to manage the business is understandable, it is worth sitting down with managers from each department and asking what they want. Producing several different types of graphs, pictures or dashboards and discussing them with managers to find the best options will help you to provide them with information that is clear and understandable.

Chapter Summary

- Technological change will have an impact on the accounting system.

- Cloud accounting – accessing the accounting system via the internet – has several benefits, including supporting home working, file sharing, multiple user access and improved sustainability. IT costs may be lower and there may be better security of data and backups.

- The risks associated with cloud accounting are the loss of control of data and security breaches over the internet, and reliance on internet access.

- Intelligent accounting software can use artificial intelligence and machine learning programmes to increase efficiency of recording day-to-day transactions. It can also audit large volumes of data and be used to create models to forecast data. However, customised machine learning programmes are costly, staff may not 'trust' the reports produced and it is hard to investigate if a mistake is thought to have occurred.

- Data analytics are software that can be used to analyse data to find out:

  - What has happened in the business? (descriptive)

  - Why did it happen? (diagnostic)

  - What is likely to happen next? (predictive)

  - What action do we need to take now? (prescriptive)

- Data analytics are costly and are used for large volumes of data.

- The operation of the accounting system is reliant on good data security. This is to ensure compliance with laws and ethics, maintain the accuracy and validity of the accounting information and to maintain operations.

- Access controls, such as passwords, authorisation to the general ledger or payroll system, and system-wide controls, such as company firewalls, must be in place to support a strong internal control system.

- Criminals may attack the accounting systems using cyberattacks (phishing, malware, ransomware) or gain access by 'hacking' into the system, either remotely or from within the business. The data and/or accounting system can also be at risk when computer equipment is lost or if data is issued in error.

- Accounting software can be used to present information to managers and clients visually, using dashboards and charts, to enable them to interpret it easily.

Key Terms		
	cloud accounting	an accounting system accessed via the internet, with information stored on a server owned by the system provider
	artificial intelligence	the concept of creating a machine that can simulate how a human thinks and behaves
	machine learning	the application of artificial intelligence that allows computers to learn from data, without explicit programming
	data analytics	the process of examining data in order to draw conclusions about the information within it
	data security	the measures in places to protect information stored on computers from unauthorised access
	cyberattack	an attempt by hackers to damage or destroy a computer network or system
	phishing	an email pretending to be from a real contact, asking for sensitive and valuable information, such as bank details
	malware	viruses attached to emails that can damage, destroy or gain entry to the computer system
	ransomware	a programme designed to lock the users out of the system and open it only once a ransom is paid
	visualisation	a method of showing the data visually that brings out its meaning eg sunburst charts
	dashboard	a type of reporting for managers and clients including pictures and graphs

Activities

5.1 Your Finance Director wants to introduce a working from home policy, using cloud accounting. You have been asked to consider the implications of this policy on the software and hardware required, as well as any possible data security issues.

Identify whether the following statements relating to implementing home working for the business are true or false.

		True/False
(a)	Cloud accounting allows several users to view information at the same time	
(b)	Hardware costs are lower with cloud accounting	
(c)	A stable internet connection is required by staff working at home	
(d)	The company will need to have a secure firewall to protect the accounting data	

5.2 Explain the common types of cyberattack.

5.3 You have been reviewing the data security policy of a business, which includes the risk to data and operations, and are aware of the following recent incidents.

Choose the correct risk for each of the following incidents. Select the risk from the following list:

Data issued in error, loss of data, malware, phishing, physical loss of equipment, ransomware, unauthorised remote access

Incident		Risk
(a)	A power cut shut down the server in the office	
(b)	An employee opened an attachment on an email from an unknown supplier	
(c)	An employee clicked on an email, which locked their computer, and was asked for cryptocurrency to unlock it	
(d)	An employee emailed a statement of account for EH Martley Ltd to EH Marley Ltd	
(e)	An employee met a friend for a meal on the way home from work. She locked her laptop in her car to keep it safe whilst in a restaurant	

5.4 Complete the following sentences for data analytics by choosing the correct option:

[**Descriptive/Diagnostic/Predictive/Prescriptive**] analytics can be used to record high volumes of data and produce monthly reports, comparing actual and budgeted information.

[**Descriptive/Diagnostic/Predictive/Prescriptive**] analytics are used to forecast future sales, using current trend information.

[**Descriptive/Diagnostic/Predictive/Prescriptive**] analytics assess the potential or new markets and products.

5.5 Your manager has been asking you to help freshen up the reporting packs for various parts of the organisation. The manager has heard about using data visualisation to help non-financial managers to understand data more easily.

Which of the following will improve the financial understanding of non-financial managers? Choose all options that apply.

(a)	Use a data dashboard, showing performance indicators	
(b)	Present information using diagrams and pictures	
(c)	Present information in an accounting format	
(d)	Ensure all financial information is included on every graph	
(e)	Produce a report in a format the manager wants	

6 Effective accounting systems

this chapter covers...

In this chapter we will look at the type of accounting systems in place for different areas of the business, looking at the internal controls within them, and how those integrated systems meet the needs of the business, by managing the risks in the business.

The accounting systems being explained are:

- *purchasing and cash payments*
- *sales and cash receipts*
- *payroll*
- *inventory*
- *capital expenditure*
- *overheads*

We will then consider how an integrated accounting system can support a strong control environment.

We will finally consider how effective systems can support ethical and sustainable practices.

WHY ARE EFFECTIVE SYSTEMS IMPORTANT?

A business needs to know that all accounting transactions that it enters into are recorded accurately and reliably. For example:

- all cash sales are recorded

- credit sales are recorded so money can be collected from customers

- business purchases are recorded and suppliers are paid for the goods

- capital items are only purchased when the business needs to buy them and they have been authorised correctly

- staff are paid for the hours they work and at the right rate

- expenses are authorised and recorded correctly

Without this accurate information, many issues could arise:

- sales may not be recorded or collected, reducing the business's profitability

- purchases could be made for individuals through the business, not for it, so fraud could occur, as people might believe the business will not notice

- inventory could be incorrectly recorded and consequently be unavailable when required, losing sales and profit for the business

- capital items could be purchased unnecessarily, incurring additional costs

- staff could be overpaid for work they have not performed, again reducing the profitability of the business

requirements of an effective system

An effective accounting system should ensure that the transactions within it are recorded:

- completely – all revenue and expenses are included

- for the sole purpose of the business – no personal items are included

- accurately – at the right value

- in the right period – only revenue or expenses that have arisen in this year should be recorded in this year

- in the right account – it is recorded either in the right general ledger account or in the correct supplier or customer account

Answering the assessment

One of the Tasks in the assessment is to review an accounting system and identify where controls may be missing or where there is potential for people to commit fraud, ie find weaknesses within it. Unless you have worked in this part of the business – accounts receivable, for example – this can be difficult to do.

To help you, most of this chapter looks at each accounting system and considers what constitutes a good system. This is important for the next chapter which covers the evaluation and review of these systems. In the final chapter, we will look at making changes, which could include introducing new controls, as part of a new system.

a short recap – internal controls

For any accounting system to be effective, there needs to be controls within it, to prevent and detect fraud and errors. We looked at this in Chapter 4 and the main types of controls are summarised below, along with an example for each:

Type of control	Example
Segregation	The Accounts Receivable Clerk, who enters invoices, cannot receive and record cash receipts
Organisation	Clear, defined roles for staff in appropriate departments, eg Finance, Production, Human Resources
Authorisation	Credit notes over £2,000 need to be authorised by the Finance Director
Physical	Petty cash tin is kept in a locked drawer
Supervision	The Management Accountant supervises the Accounts Payable Clerk to ensure duties are carried out to the required standard
Personnel	Qualified, competent staff
Arithmetical and Accounting	The wages control account is reconciled regularly
Management	Management accounts are produced and reviewed each month, with variances investigated

We are now going to consider each accounting system in turn looking at:

- the elements of the system, stating what happens within it

- the requirements of the system for it to be effective (known as control objectives)

- potential risks ie fraud and errors that could occur if adequate controls are not in place

- the control procedures in place in an effective system, including the information required for it to operate

THE PURCHASES AND PAYMENTS SYSTEM

system elements

The diagram below shows the elements of a basic purchases and payments system. (Note that internal controls are shown in italics.)

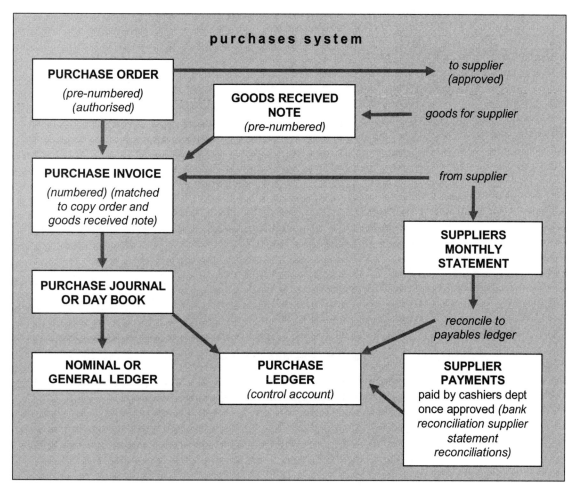

Within this system there are several internal controls. The system works broadly as follows:

■ the purchase order will be raised by the buying department. It should be authorised by someone who has the authority to purchase goods or services on behalf of the company and it must be within their authorisation limit. It may be generated based on a quotation requested by a budget holder and will include price, quantity and delivery date information

■ orders should be pre-numbered so that the company can control their issue. A copy will be sent to the accounts department and another copy to the goods inward department to tell them to expect a delivery

■ the purchase order will also be sent to a supplier who has previously been approved by the company. This approval means the supplier is considered reliable and able to deliver goods or services of the right quality, on time and at the agreed price

■ when the goods are received, they will be checked for quality and quantity by the goods inwards or inventory control staff and compared and agreed to the order. Details of the items received will be entered into the inventory records

■ goods inwards staff will issue a pre-numbered goods received note and send a copy to the accounts department

■ when the invoice from the supplier arrives, the accounts department will agree the details to its copy of the purchase order, including the price and quantity, along with the goods received note. This will ensure that the goods were ordered properly and priced and that the company has actually received them

■ once matched and arithmetically checked, the invoice can be entered into the purchases day book or journal and from there to the nominal or general ledger and the payables ledger

■ a monthly statement from the supplier will be reconciled to the balance on the payables ledger account to ensure all invoices, credit notes and payments have been properly recorded. This 'third party' confirmation is an excellent check for this

On receipt of the supplier statement, and once the purchase invoice has been approved for payment and falls due, it will be paid.

In addition to the internal controls detailed above, the principle of segregation of duties applies in this system. The individuals who carry out each stage of the process should all be different so that no one individual can be involved with the whole transaction. This reduces the risk of errors or fraud on the part of the member of staff. A different person should ideally do each of the following:

■ order goods

■ deal with the movement (receipt) of goods

- process invoices
- pay the invoices

control objectives for the purchases and cash payments system

To re-cap – there are five main sections of the purchase system:

- placing the order
- receiving the goods
- receiving the invoice from the supplier
- recording the transaction in the accounts
- paying the invoice

Control objectives are statements that address how an organisation will manage risks to it. The control objectives for purchases can be identified for each stage of the purchases system as follows:

ordering

- only goods and services required by the business are ordered
- all orders for goods and services are properly authorised
- orders are made only from approved suppliers

receipt of goods

- all goods and services received are for the purposes of the business and not for private use
- only goods and services that have been ordered are accepted
- goods ordered are received in a satisfactory condition
- unsatisfactory goods are returned to suppliers
- all receipts of goods and services are accurately recorded
- receipt of goods or services is evidenced

receipt of invoice

- liabilities are recognised for all goods and services received
- all invoices received are authorised
- any credits due to the business for faulty goods and services have been claimed
- liabilities cannot be recorded for goods or services which have not been received or approved

accounting for purchases

- all expenditure is correctly recorded in the books and records of the business

- all credit notes are properly recorded in the books and records of the business
- all entries in the purchases ledger are to the correct suppliers' accounts
- all entries in the general ledger are to the correct account
- all purchases are recorded in the correct accounting period

payment

- all payments have been properly authorised
- all payments are for goods and services which have been received

potential risks if purchase system controls are not in place

If the system of internal control is weak and the internal controls are not working, this increases the risk of some or all of the following:

- purchasing goods and services the company does not need
- failing to buy goods and services of the appropriate quality and at the lowest cost
- buying from unauthorised suppliers
- loss of discounts or bulk buying opportunities
- orders being placed by staff who are not authorised to do so
- orders being duplicated, either fraudulently or in error
- goods received not being checked for quality and quantity or accepted when not ordered
- fraud through the processing of false invoices or fraudulent payments
- invoices not being checked for receipt of order before being paid
- invoices being paid twice or not being paid at all, which may result in loss of supplier confidence
- poor cash flow if invoices are paid without taking advantage of credit terms and discounts
- incorrect inventory records
- purchases and trade payables not being recorded accurately in the financial records
- incorrect period end procedures

purchases and cash payments system controls

Now that we have identified the requirements of the purchases system, and the risks of fraud and error, we can examine the controls, information and procedures that the system should have in place to ensure that these requirements are achieved and also to minimise the risk of fraud and error.

Throughout the whole purchase process there should be formal written procedures for ordering, receiving and paying for goods and services.

Another key control within the system is segregation of duties – there should ideally be separate staff responsible for raising orders, receiving goods, and approving and paying invoices.

ordering

organisational controls	– ordering is only allowed from approved suppliers, accessed and set up only by specified individuals within the organisation
physical controls	– blank order forms are kept secure
authorisation	– there are recognised authority levels for orders above defined limits
	– where purchase orders are computer-generated, only authorised individuals, using secure logins, are able to do so
arithmetic and accounting checks	– standard pre-numbered order forms are always used, stating quantity, price, delivery details
	– regular review of orders placed but not received

receipt of goods

physical controls	– quantity and condition of goods received are properly checked
	– pre-numbered goods received notes (GRNs) are always used stating quantity, description, date received, condition
authorisation	– GRNs are signed off for all goods received
	– GRNs are matched to the order, which has been authorised

receipt of invoice and accounting

organisational controls	– stated authority levels should exist for approving invoices
authorisation	– all invoices are approved for payment

arithmetic and *accounting checks*	–	invoices are matched with orders and GRNs
	–	prices on invoices are agreed to standard supplier price lists, discounts and order forms
	–	arithmetical accuracy of invoices is checked and evidenced
	–	regular reconciliations of suppliers' statements with payables ledger balances for accurate supplier account information
	–	controls exist for processing purchase invoices (eg batch totals)
	–	regular reconciliations of payables ledger control account with purchases ledger balances and reconciling items investigated and cleared
	–	period end checks are performed to ensure goods received but not invoiced are accounted for in the correct period

payment

physical controls	–	cheque books are securely located
	–	bank passwords are secure and not shared
	–	cancelled cheques are retained
authorisation	–	recognised list of authorised cheque signatories or BACS approvals
	–	a minimum of two signatories for all payments or approvals for BACS or cheque payments at appropriate management levels
arithmetic and *accounting checks*	–	regular bank reconciliation performed comparing cash book to bank statements, with reconciling items investigated and cleared

Note: The bank reconciliation between the cash book and bank statements is an excellent way to ensure the cash book is complete and accurate, as the comparison is with a third party, ie the bank.

purchases of expenses

The purchases system described above is for when the business is buying goods. However, sometimes the company will incur costs for which it will be invoiced which are for services, and these are most likely to be expenses, or overhead costs. This could include costs such as rent, rates, legal services, equipment rental, consultancy fees, travel, etc.

control objectives for the purchases of expenses

The control objectives outlined for purchases on pages 101-102, excluding the receipts of goods, also apply for expenses.

potential risks if controls for purchases of expenses are not in place

Similarly, the potential risks if controls for purchases of expenses are not in place on page 102 apply, excluding those for receiving goods.

purchases of expenses controls

The purchasing procedures should still include the type of internal controls you would expect within an ordinary purchasing system, such as authorisation of orders, but you will obviously not be able to match orders to Goods Received Notes to ensure goods have been delivered.

Therefore, you will need to look closely to see if the following controls are in place.

authorisation	– Budget holders will be able to order services and they should be of an appropriate level eg managers or senior managers.
	– These are set authorisation limits, eg Budget holder up to £10,000, Department Director over £10,000.
	– Budget holders authorise the invoice, using set authorisation limits as before.
	– Expenses payments are authorised by at least two people eg Finance Director and one other.
segregation	– The Budget Holder or Director authorises the order.
	– Accounts Payable contacts the supplier for payment details.
	– Payments made are authorised by two appropriate personnel, eg one Director and one senior manager.
accounting and arithmetic checks	– Orders will be sequentially numbered and accounts will issue the order number and inform the budget holder of it.
	– Invoices will be entered onto the invoice register when they come into accounts and will be sequentially numbered, prior to sending to the Budget Holder or Director for authorisation.

– Only when invoices are authorised by the appropriate person are they are posted to the purchases ledger.

– All expenses payments made are supported by the invoice and any other supporting documentation.

management

– Management accounts are produced monthly and variances of expenses expenditure are investigated.

THE SALES AND CASH RECEIPTS SYSTEM

system elements

The diagram below shows the elements of a basic credit sales system.

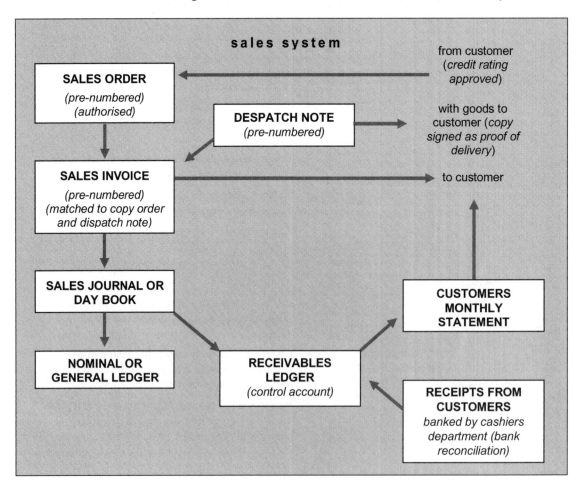

Within this system there are several internal controls. The system will work broadly like this:

- the sales orders will be taken by a sales department who will confirm the credit-worthiness of the customer with the accounts department

- goods will be despatched to the customer with a delivery note by the staff who deal with inventories and goods outwards. A copy of the delivery note will be signed by the customer and retained by the company as proof that the goods were delivered

- the sales invoice and the customer statement will be raised by the accounts department

- the accounts department will post the sales invoice to the sales daybook or to a journal. From there they will post it to the receivables ledger and the nominal or general ledger

- when the customer pays the invoice, the money received will be banked and recorded in the cash book by the accounts department. It is important to ensure that the individuals who process sales invoices do not also process the monies received from customers

- outstanding trade receivables balances will be reviewed to identify any possible irrecoverable or doubtful receivables and to chase slow payers

As in the purchases system, the principle of segregation of duties also applies to this system. The individuals who carry out each stage of the process should be different, so that no one individual can be involved with the whole transaction.

control objectives of the sales and cash receipts system

As with purchases there are five main sections of the sales system:

- receiving the order (and granting credit)
- despatching the goods
- raising the invoice
- recording the transactions in the accounts
- receiving payment

The control objectives, or requirements, can be identified for each stage of the sales system as follows:

receiving the order (and granting credit)

- goods and services are only supplied to customers on credit if their credit rating is good and they are within their credit limits

- orders are recorded correctly when they are received

despatching the goods

- goods are only despatched on the basis of approved orders
- all despatches of goods and services are accurately recorded
- all returns from customers are recorded and the reasons for rejection are investigated

invoicing

- all invoices raised relate to goods and services supplied by the business
- all despatches of goods or provision of services are invoiced at the correct price and on authorised terms
- credit notes are authorised and only issued for a valid reason

accounting for sales

- all sales are properly recorded in the books and records of the organisation
- all credit notes issued are properly recorded in the books and records of the organisation
- all entries in the receivables ledger are to the correct customer accounts
- all entries in the general ledger are to the correct account
- all sales have been recorded in the correct accounting period
- procedures exist for identifying irrecoverable receivables

receiving payment (receipts)

- all receipts from customers have been properly recorded
- all payments received are for goods and services which have been supplied

potential risks if sales system controls are not in place

If the internal control objectives are not being met, then there is an increased risk of the following occurring in the business:

- selling to non-creditworthy customers
- failure to record customer orders and therefore supplying incorrect or incomplete orders, or not supplying at all and losing a sales opportunity
- goods or services being supplied without being invoiced
- duplication of sales invoices

- sales invoices not being checked before despatch, and issued with incorrect figures

- incorrect VAT calculations

- goods and services sold at the wrong price

- credit notes being issued for something other than goods returned, for example fraudulently writing off debts

- incorrect inventory records, despatches not being recorded correctly or theft of inventory not being detected

- poor credit control resulting in weak cash management

- sales and receivables not being recorded accurately and correctly in the financial records

- theft of money received from customers

- incorrect cut-off procedures

sales and cash receipts system controls

Now that we have identified the control objectives of the sales system, we can examine the controls information and procedures that the system should have in place to ensure that these requirements are achieved and also to minimise the risk of fraud and error.

In businesses where sales involve a significant number of cash transactions, there is an increased risk of fraud, and senior management have to be very aware of this. For this reason, cash sales will be dealt with separately at the end of this section. Where sales are made online, some controls are particularly important and this is highlighted at the end of this section as well.

Throughout the sales process there should be formal written procedures for receiving orders, granting credit, despatching goods and collecting payment for goods and services supplied.

There should also be segregation of duties within the system with different staff responsible for taking orders, granting credit, despatching goods and receiving payment.

receiving orders and granting credit

organisational controls	–	there are recognised authority levels for accepting new customers
	–	procedures are in place to credit check all new customers and increases in credit limits for existing customers
physical controls	–	blank sales order forms are kept secure

authorisation	–	there are recognised authority levels for changes in customer data (eg increasing discounts allowed)
	–	all increases to customer credit limits are authorised
arithmetic and accounting checks	–	pre-numbered sales order forms are always used stating quantity, price, description, delivery details, discounts
	–	prices quoted to customers are checked to standard price list and appropriate discounts applied

despatching goods

organisational controls	–	delivery notes are matched with orders and invoices
physical controls	–	the quantity and condition of goods supplied are properly checked
	–	pre-numbered delivery notes should always be used
	–	proof of delivery is obtained for all goods despatched (signed delivery notes)
	–	returns from customers are recorded (pre-numbered goods returned notes issued by the buyer) and reasons investigated

invoicing and accounting for revenue

organisational controls	–	invoices and credit notes are pre numbered and sequentially issued, and spoilt invoices are not destroyed
authorisation	–	all credit notes are authorised
	–	all non-standard discounts are approved
arithmetic and accounting checks	–	invoices are matched with orders and delivery notes
	–	prices on invoices are agreed to standard price lists or appropriate costing information and discount information
	–	VAT rates are verified on the invoice
	–	credit notes are matched with goods returned notes and the reason recorded

–   controls are in place for processing invoices (eg batch totals)

–   invoices and credit notes are entered into the accounting records promptly

–   invoices and credit notes are posted to the correct customer account

–   regular up-to-date statements are sent to customers

–   regular reconciliation of the receivables ledger control account with receivables ledger balances

–   period end checks are performed to ensure goods that have been despatched but not invoiced are accounted for in the correct period

receiving payment (receipts)

physical controls

–   all money received from customers is initially recorded by two people

–   all money received is banked intact on the same day using paying in slips

arithmetic and accounting checks

–   regular bank reconciliations are performed comparing the cash book and bank statement and investigating differences using paying in slips, BACS records etc

–   all cash received is posted to the correct customer account

cash sales system

There are certain types of business where a significant volume of sales is received in cash. Examples include supermarkets, bars, restaurants, taxi firms and hairdressers. You will be able to think of others.

When designing procedures for these types of organisations, the directors or senior management have to consider the increased likelihood of fraud. Inadequate controls in the sales system over the collection and recording of cash receipts could lead to misappropriation of cash.

Consequently, there are additional controls that need to be in place to ensure the accuracy of the recording of cash sales and the certainty that all of them have been recorded.

Additional controls for cash sales include:

■   all cash sales to be recorded using a till (credit card sales would also be recorded here under a separate category)

- authorised staff perform a daily cash count at the end of the day and ensure the correct amount is entered onto daily takings sheet

- daily takings sheet matching the cash sales per the till receipt to the cash banked to be completed

- differences between cash sales per the till and cash to be banked to be investigated

- if cash is held overnight, it is kept in a secure locked location, eg a safe

- cash receipts to be banked intact (ie with no cash payments made from them) daily

- if any items, such as wages, small bills or petty cash items are paid out of cash, they are to be supported with documentation (receipts, timesheet etc) and a reconciliation of till cash to the amount of cash banked to be completed

online sales system

Many businesses now have websites where customers can look at products and place orders directly. A good website will make it easy for customers to place orders, pay and give estimated or exact delivery information.

The website often links directly into the sales ordering part of the system, so orders can be placed by the customer and the use of discount codes is common. 'Cash' customers, who pay on order, often pay using a credit card, using a payment system such as 'Paypal'.

Strong controls must be in place when goods are picked from the warehouse and despatched. If someone ordered a computer costing £500, but one costing £700 was accidentally despatched, it could be time-consuming and difficult for the company to get the product returned, particularly if the customer bought it as a 'one-off', so was unlikely to make a purchase again.

When items are posted or couriered to the customer, there is a risk of a customer saying the goods have not arrived and asking for a refund, so obtaining proof of delivery is essential.

As customers who buy online have the right to change their mind and return the goods, the controls over the returns and refunds process should be robust.

Additional controls for online sales are:

- only authorised personnel can update and issue discount codes for use online

- use an online payment system that authorises the credit card payment prior to the order being accepted

- daily reconciliation of online payments to bank payments, to identify if any credit card chargebacks are made, prior to orders being despatched

- confirm the order is paid for, prior to despatch

- have an authorisation policy and process in place for online returns. Legally, the customer must inform the business within 14 days of the delivery and the goods must be returned 14 days after that.

THE PAYROLL SYSTEM

The payroll system contains details of the organisation's staff and their wages and salary payments. The organisation's requirements when operating the payroll system are to ensure that it pays the correct rate of pay for the actual amount of work done.

The principal differences between wages and salaries are:

- wages tend to be paid weekly and salaries monthly

- wages can vary from week to week, whereas salaries are generally a set payment, and only vary if commission or bonus payments are included

It is becoming increasingly rare for wages to be paid in cash; for security reasons most staff are paid directly into their bank account by BACS. If payments are still made in cash, there are a number of issues that are raised which we will look at later in this section.

Key points that relate to both wages and salaries are:

- all employees must have a contract or written terms of employment

- rates of pay must be agreed

- all deductions from gross pay must be statutory (eg PAYE and NIC) or authorised by the employee (eg pension contributions)

- there are defined rules for calculating tax and National Insurance contributions, whatever method is used for paying staff

- staff must be paid regularly and on time

- payroll must comply with taxation rules eg real time information for HMRC

Businesses may have a mixture of staff paid a weekly wage and staff paid a monthly salary. In this case they may operate two payrolls. If this is the case, directors must ensure information requirements are met and controls are in place for each payroll to ensure that both are operated correctly.

confidentiality

In Chapter 3 we explained how accounts staff must treat all the information they have access to on a day-to-day basis as confidential. This is particularly important when dealing with payroll. Matters such as rates of pay and individual's salaries can be an extremely sensitive area and one that can be of particular interest to other employees!

The payroll system contains much personal information about employees, including:

- the hourly rate of pay or annual salary

- additional benefits

- home address

- bank details

- date of birth

- National Insurance number

It is the duty of the organisation under the Data Protection Act 2018 to ensure that all this information remains confidential.

system elements

The diagram below shows the components of a basic payroll system, whether for wages or salaries. (Internal controls are shown in italics.)

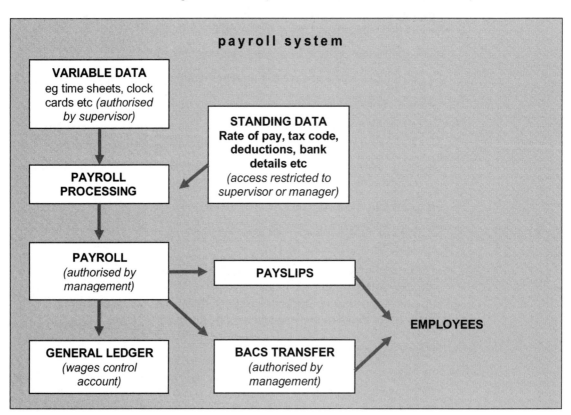

In contrast to the purchases and sales systems we have looked at, there is a limited segregation of duties within a payroll system as, normally, the payroll is prepared by staff in one department who carry out the entire process.

The actual payment of wages or salaries is made by the accounts department but it is the payroll staff who tell them how much to pay to whom.

The key controls in the payroll system are authorisation and management review.

The system works broadly like this:

- variable data such as overtime or hours worked for casual workers is approved by a manager based on some form of time recording. This could be a clock card or a time sheet. The hours to be paid should be validated and authorised before being input to the payroll system

- salaried staff who are not paid overtime are paid a regular amount each month. Any additional payments such as bonuses or commission should also be authorised

- the computer will contain a master file which contains fixed data about each employee. Such data includes:
  - staff number
  - rate of pay (hourly, weekly, monthly)
  - tax code
  - National Insurance (NI) number
  - deductions such as pension contributions, subscriptions, student loans, court orders etc
  - bank details – sort code and account number

- the payroll software applies the variable data to the standing data and calculates:
  - gross pay
  - deductions (PAYE, NIC, others as notified)
  - net pay
  - gross taxable pay to date
  - tax paid to date

- the payroll software prepares and reports real time information (RTI) to HMRC

- the software also prepares a payments list; in most cases employees are paid by automatic bank transfers using the Banks Automated Credit System (BACS)

- payslips are prepared to be sent to each employee

- the payroll should be approved by management

- the BACS payment list must be signed ideally by two authorised signatories

- payment is made by direct transfer originated by the accounts department

control objectives of the payroll system

The main stages of the payroll system are as follows:

- hours are input into the system as required and amendments to staff details are made when necessary

- gross pay, deductions and net pay are calculated and payslips produced

- transactions are recorded in the accounts

- payments are made to staff and HM Revenue & Customs

The control objectives for the system can be identified for each stage of the system as follows:

inputting hours and amending staff details

- all amendments to staff details are properly authorised

- hours worked are approved at an appropriate level

- staff are only paid for hours worked

- only staff who work for the business are included on the payroll

- details of leavers and joiners are authorised and promptly entered onto the payroll system

- staff details remain confidential at all times

calculating payroll and deductions

- payroll is calculated based on approved rates and hours worked

- statutory deductions for PAYE and NIC are correctly calculated

- voluntary deductions (eg pension contributions or share save schemes) are correctly calculated

- RTI is accurate and reported to HMRC within required deadlines

accounting for payroll and payments to staff and HM Revenue & Customs

- net pay is accurately calculated and paid to the correct employee

- payroll figures are correctly recorded in the books and records of the business, including pension contributions, share save schemes, etc

- all payments for PAYE and NIC are paid on the due date

- wages and salaries are paid on the right date

potential risks if payroll system controls are not in place

The risks to, or impact on, the business if the controls are not working are:

- paying for work which has not been carried out

- incorrect gross pay calculation

- paying people who are not employees, ie those who have left the business

- failure to pay new employees

- failure to pay wages and salaries on the correct date

- incorrect calculation of net pay

- failing to deduct correct amounts of tax and National Insurance

- failure to report RTI due to HMRC on time, leading to fines

- failure to pay amounts due to HMRC on time, leading to fines

- paying 'ghost' workers ie fictitious employees fraudulently included on payroll

- amounts for wages and salaries incorrectly recorded in financial records

payroll system controls

We can now examine the controls information and procedures that the system should have in place to ensure that these information requirements are achieved and the risk of fraud and error minimised.

Throughout the whole payroll process there should be formal written procedures for recording and inputting hours worked, amending staff details, and paying wages and salaries.

There should also be segregation of duties between staff responsible for approving hours worked, making changes to staff details and inputting and calculating payments. Where wages are paid in cash, one person should be responsible for counting the cash and another more senior person should check the amounts paid.

inputting hours and amending staff details

organisational controls
- a written record such as a contract of employment is kept for each employee containing details of rates of pay and contracted hours; any changes should require appropriate authorisation
- formal procedures are followed for starters and leavers

	– timesheets and clock cards are approved before hours are entered onto the payroll system
physical controls	– access to the payroll office is restricted to authorised personnel only
	– access to the payroll and staff records is restricted to authorised personnel only
authorisation	– all changes to rates of pay, bonus payments and commission earned should be authorised
	– written approval from employees should be obtained for all voluntary deductions from wages or salaries
arithmetic and accounting controls	– all timesheets to be added up to ensure accuracy

calculating payroll and deductions

organisational controls	– up-to-date versions of payroll software should be installed, using the latest tax and National Insurance rates, which are RTI-compliant
	– staff are fully trained on PAYE and NI issues
	– changes to staff tax codes are promptly and accurately entered on the payroll system
authorisation	– payroll schedules are approved before payment
arithmetic and accounting checks	– wages and salaries control account is regularly reconciled
	– commission and bonuses are reconciled to source documentation (eg sales records)
	– piecework payments (ie payments based on the number of items produced) are regularly reviewed against levels of work completed
	– unusual changes in payments to individuals from month to month are identified

accounting for payroll and payments to staff and HM Revenue & Customs

organisational controls	– a timetable for payment of wages and salaries is maintained and adhered to
physical controls	– staff who count wages in cash are not the same as those who prepare the payroll
	– at least two staff handle cash for wages
	– cash for payment of wages is stored securely at all times
	– payslips are given to staff members personally, emailed to them securely or posted to their home address
authorisation	– pay packets can only be signed for by the individual staff member
	– BACS payment schedules are authorised by an appropriate person before processing
arithmetic and accounting checks	– the wages control account is regularly reconciled
	– a comparison is made between wages paid and budgeted figures for wages by department
	– a regular check is made of deductions by accounts staff to ensure consistency with previous periods' deductions
	– reconciliations are regularly performed between the total net pay figure and payment shown on the bank statement
	– a regular review of National Insurance and PAYE accounts to ensure no outstanding balances remain after payment to HM Revenue & Customs
	– a regular review of other payroll accounts, such as pension contributions due, to ensure no outstanding balances remain after payments made

INVENTORY SYSTEM

system components

The diagram below shows the elements of a basic inventory system. *(Internal controls are shown in italics.)*

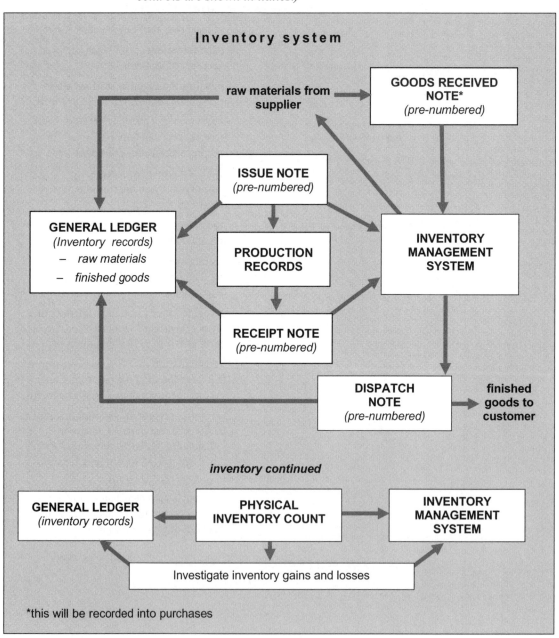

Within this system there are a number of internal controls. The system works broadly like this:

- the business will use an inventory management system to order inventory when required and record receipts of raw materials, booking these into stores

- direct materials will be issued from stores to production, when required

- when finished, production will be transferred to stores into finished goods in the inventory management system

- finished goods are despatched and removed from the inventory management system

- the inventory management system updates the inventory records in the general ledger

- periodically the physical inventory is reconciled to the inventory management system and the inventory records in the general ledger

As mentioned in the previous systems, segregation of duties is important. Those who control the inventory system should not physically count the inventory and investigate differences.

control objectives of the inventory system

There are four main sections of the system, usually controlled by an Inventory Management System:

- ordering and receiving inventory from suppliers

- booking inventory in and out of stores (ie the warehouse)

- despatching goods to customers

- reconciling and investigating the differences between physical inventory, the Inventory Management System and the general ledger

The control objectives for each stage of the inventory system can be identified as follows:

ordering and receiving inventory from suppliers

- materials or items ordered for production or sales are authorised, to ensure they are necessary

- materials or items ordered for production or sales are inspected on delivery to ensure they are of appropriate quality and complete

- materials or items received are accurately booked into stores as inventory

- materials or items are stored securely
- all inventory is accurately booked in and out of stores
- goods are despatched to customers accurately
- physical inventory is periodically compared to the inventory management records and the general ledger to ensure the accuracy of the booking in and out, receiving and despatching procedures

booking inventory in and out of stores

- all inventory is accurately booked in and out of stores

despatching goods to customers

- goods are despatched to customers accurately, using an authorised customer order
- all despatched items are accurately record using goods despatched notes
- despatched goods are removed from inventory

reconciling and investigating the differences between physical inventory, the inventory management system and the general ledger

- the physical inventory matches that in the inventory management system and the general ledger
- inventory is valued appropriately in the inventory management system and the general ledger, including obsolete or scrap inventory
- all differences between the inventory management system and the general ledger are calculated and reasons investigated

potential risks if the inventory system controls are not in place

If the internal controls are not working, then there is an increased risk of the following:

- unnecessary items may be ordered
- unnecessary items may be received which have not been ordered
- materials may be received which are of unsatisfactory quality or quantity
- inventory records could be inaccurate, causing production delays
- inventory could be stolen
- inventory could be damaged
- 'good' inventory could be scrapped unnecessarily

- sales could be unfulfilled due to a lack of inventory

- cost of sales and the value of inventory could be recorded inaccurately and incorrectly in the financial records

inventory system controls

Now that we have looked at the requirements of an inventory system, we can examine the controls, information and procedures that the system should have in place to ensure these requirements are achieved and also to minimise the risk of fraud and error.

Throughout the inventory system there should be formal written procedures for inventory management, booking items in and out of stores, despatching goods to customers and the process of inventory counts and reconciling it to the general ledger.

There should be segregation of duties within the system with different staff responsible for receiving inventory, controlling inventory and investigating differences in physical inventory, the inventory management system and the general ledger.

ordering and receiving inventory from suppliers

organisational controls	– there are written procedures for the purchase of inventory required by the inventory management system
	– there are written procedures for the receipt of inventory into stores
physical controls	– inventory received is matched to an authorised purchase order
	– the quality and condition of goods supplied are properly checked on delivery
	– returns to suppliers are recorded (pre-numbered goods returned notes) and reasons investigated
arithmetic and accounting checks	– goods received are recorded into inventory using sequentially numbered goods received notes

booking inventory in and out of stores

organisational controls	– there are written procedures for the issue of inventory to and from stores and the inventory management system
physical controls	– inventory is stored in a secure location, accessed only by the stores staff
	– inventory is housed appropriately, to keep it in good condition
	– goods received notes are issued with each delivery
arithmetic and accounting checks	– issue notes for inventory from stores to production have a unique, sequential number
	– receipt notes for inventory into stores from production have a unique, sequential number

despatching goods to customers

organisational controls	– goods despatched notes (delivery notes) are matched to the sales order
arithmetic and accounting checks	– automatic updating of the despatch in the inventory system and the general ledger

reconciling and investigating the differences between physical inventory, the inventory management system and the general ledger

organisational controls	– there are written procedures for the inventory count, where two people count together, independent from stores/the warehouse. Inventory sheets are pre-numbered with no quantities shown
	– there are recognised procedures for investigating inventory gains and losses (the difference between the inventory management system and physical inventory)

physical controls	– no receipts or despatches are made during the inventory count; the last goods received note and goods despatch note numbers are recorded
	– no inventory is moved around the factory whilst the inventory count is performed
	– items are marked as counted, to avoid both double counting and not counting items
	– all inventory sheets issued are accounted for before the inventory count is finished
	– a physical review of each location by a manager, to ensure items are marked as counted, will be undertaken
arithmetic and accounting checks	– periodical inventory counts are performed matching physical items to the inventory records and vice versa to confirm the existence of inventory and the accuracy of the records
	– regular reconciliation of inventory system to general ledger
	– the gross profit margin is reviewed periodically to ensure it is at expected levels
management	– all significant gains and losses are investigated by appropriately senior, qualified staff

CAPITAL EXPENDITURE (NON-CURRENT ASSETS) SYSTEM

system elements

When a business is considering purchasing a non-current asset, it is investing in its future, so the capital expenditure process is slightly different, as shown in the diagram that follows. (Note that internal controls are shown in italics.)

As you can see, the capital expenditure system differs from the purchases system in two main areas – initial approval and purchase and the non-current asset register, used for recording and the ongoing control of the non-current assets. Therefore, we will just focus on these two different areas.

approval and purchase

The capital expenditure approval system is different, as the items being bought could be for several thousands of pounds.

- As part of the budgeting process, in order to ensure the business really needs the item being purchased, management will look at how they plan to meet the future needs of the business in terms of plant, equipment, machinery, buildings and vehicles for the short, medium and longer term. Initially they will usually consider up to five years of potential investment, with a detailed capital expenditure budget for the first year.

- If the business is a limited company, the capital expenditure budget will normally be approved by the Board of Directors, prior to the start of the year.

- Non-current assets are authorised by being included in the capital expenditure budget. They are likely to be purchased either from an approved supplier or by a tendering process, with a minimum of three suppliers being considered, to ensure the price and service will be as the business requires. Once a supplier is agreed on, a purchase order will be raised as in the purchases system.

- Non-current assets may take time to install, before they start being used. It is important the non-current assets are properly inspected and in working order before they are paid for.

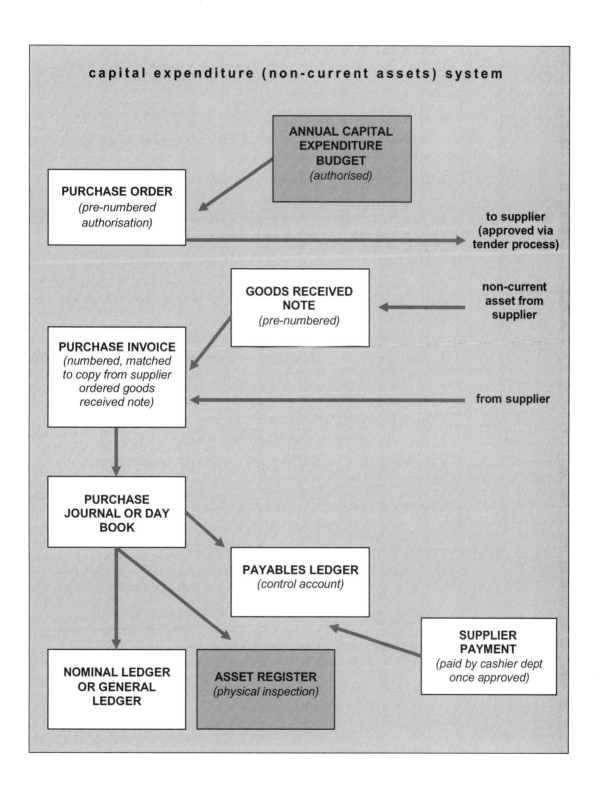

capital expenditure (non-current assets) system

ANNUAL CAPITAL EXPENDITURE BUDGET
(authorised)

PURCHASE ORDER
(pre-numbered authorisation)

to supplier (approved via tender process)

GOODS RECEIVED NOTE
(pre-numbered)

non-current asset from supplier

PURCHASE INVOICE
(numbered, matched to copy from supplier ordered goods received note)

from supplier

PURCHASE JOURNAL OR DAY BOOK

PAYABLES LEDGER
(control account)

SUPPLIER PAYMENT
(paid by cashier dept once approved)

NOMINAL LEDGER OR GENERAL LEDGER

ASSET REGISTER
(physical inspection)

control objectives for non-current asset approval & purchase

The control objectives for approving and purchasing non-current assets, including those in the purchases system discussed above, are:

- Only non-current assets that are required by the business are approved

- Non-current assets are purchased from approved suppliers for the best price

- Non-current assets are in working order, prior to being paid for

potential risks if the capital expenditure approval and purchase controls are not in place

If the internal controls in the capital expenditure approval system are not in place, including those in the purchases system discussed above, this increases the risk of some or all of the following:

- purchasing capital items that the business does not need

- failing to buy capital items of the appropriate quality and at the lowest cost

- buying from unauthorised suppliers

- loss of discount opportunities

- orders being placed by staff who are not authorised to do so

- capital items being paid for when they are not working properly

approval and purchase controls

The controls within the approval and purchase part of the system, in addition to those in the purchases system, are listed below:

organisational controls	–	ordering is by a tendering process, using approved suppliers
authorisation	–	the Board approves the capital expenditure budget for the year, as part of a five year or longer plan
	–	the purchase order is approved in line with capital expenditure authorisation budget
physical	–	the non-current asset is thoroughly inspected and is in working order prior to being paid for

asset register

Once a capital item has been received and invoiced, it will be entered in the general ledger as a non-current asset. A detailed non-current asset register will be kept, recording the following:

- purchase date
- supplier
- unique reference number (item may be barcoded – see below)
- cost
- useful life
- depreciation rate, depreciation charged to date
- location/department
- responsible manager/employee

The non-current asset register forms the main record for non-current assets for the business. As it is so detailed, it can be used for controlling movements of these assets and for ensuring they are all still held by the company.

In a large organisation, where there are many types and classes of non-current assets, non-current assets might be barcoded and recorded on a non-current asset management system. In a smaller business, the non-current asset register may be a spreadsheet.

Periodically, the business will compare all the physical items with the non-current asset register and the accounting records, following up any differences. This is the same principle as reconciling physical inventory and the inventory records. For non-current assets, it could take several weeks. Barcoding or unique reference numbers may enable this comparison process to be as fast and efficient as possible.

Finally, when non-current assets are disposed of, there should be an authorisation process in place, so only authorised people are able to make the sale and then update the records. You would not want anyone to be able to sell the company's factory!

control objectives for non-current asset register

The control objectives for the non-current asset register are as follows:

- all non-current asset are recorded accurately and at the correct value in the non-current asset register and the general ledger
- non-current assets are held securely
- all depreciation calculations are accurate
- all disposals are made with appropriate authorisation and the non-current asset register is updated accurately

■ the financial statements accurately reflect the correct non-current asset information, depreciation expense and disposal information

asset register controls

The controls relating to the asset register are set out below:

authorisation	–	disposal of assets and removal from the non-current asset register will be approved by authorised people
physical	–	assets are barcoded and secured where possible
	–	ownership documents are securely stored
arithmetic and accounting	–	regular reconciliation of the asset register to physical assets held and differences investigated
	–	reconciliation of asset register to general or nominal ledger on a regular basis eg monthly for cost, depreciation and carrying value

potential risks if non-current asset register controls are not in place

If the internal controls in the non-current asset register part of the non-current asset system are not in place, this increases the risk of some or all of the following:

■ incorrect non-current asset records in the general ledger

■ capital items being misplaced or removed from the company

■ inaccurate depreciation calculations, resulting in inaccurate profits

■ disposals being made without appropriate authorisation and at a below market value

■ the financial statements not reflecting the correct non-current asset information, depreciation expense and disposal information

THE VALUE OF AN INTEGRATED SYSTEM

integration and authorisation

A well organised system should ideally be an integrated computerised system on a network using proprietary software such as Sage and Microsoft Office. All the accounting systems should integrate (link) together, so the general ledger is up to date and accurate. Information should only need to be entered manually once, reducing the risk of errors or fraud.

As the whole system is linked, the business should consider who should be able to see what. As previously stated, segregation is critical to minimising the risk of fraud, so people should only be given access to those parts of the system needed to do their job effectively. To maintain this, accounting staff will have their own passwords authorising which areas of the system they can access. For example, the Payroll Clerk should be able to access the payroll system but not the general ledger or cashbook. These passwords should be kept confidential and be of a secure nature – often passwords now must contain letters, numbers, lower and upper case items and unusual characters. Wag3s!pa4 would be a strong password, as long as it is not written on a post-it next to the Payroll Clerk's desk!

reporting and monitoring using an integrated system

Where a system is integrated, data can be extracted very easily and in a prompt and user-friendly manner. This allows the business to monitor its activities well and to produce reports as and when necessary. For example, payroll could be analysed by department or by job, to see where efficiencies might be made. The business can produce management accounts promptly and take corrective or preventative action to improve future performance.

An integrated system can also assist in meeting the needs of other stakeholders. For example, customers want invoicing to be prompt and accurate, with accurate monthly statements, clearly showing payments they have made and an integrated revenue system will give this. Similarly, suppliers require accurate information, so all invoices will be correctly recorded and the ledger accurately reflects their transactions with the business.

HOW EFFECTIVE SYSTEMS CAN SUPPORT ETHICAL PRACTICE AND SUSTAINABILITY

ethical considerations

A system with strong internal controls can not only be effective in recording and controlling the transactions of the company, it can also support ethical values. By having controls in place, it can ensure ethical principles are met on a daily basis.

The relevant ethical principles as explained on pages 45-48 are:

- Objectivity
- Integrity

- Professional Behaviour
- Professional Competence and Due Care
- Confidentiality

Examples of some different systems, the controls within them and how they support ethical principles (in italics) are shown below:

payroll	–	only payroll staff can access staff data *(confidentiality)*
	–	wages can only be collected by the person being paid and are signed for *(professional competence and due care)*
sales	–	credit limits are set using a credit control policy *(objectivity)*
	–	overdue debts are chased according to a detailed credit control policy for all customers *(objectivity)*
	–	discounts are applied according to company policy and communicated to customers *(integrity)*
	–	credit control staff are trained to deal with late payers in an appropriate manner and following the credit control policy *(professional behaviour)*
purchases	–	the tendering process is clear and specified *(professional behaviour, objectivity)*
	–	when goods are received they are compared to the order and the physical condition of them is checked *(professional competence and due care)*
	–	supplier payments are made in line with supplier terms *(integrity)*

sustainable considerations

Just as an effective system can support ethical practice, it can also support sustainability. For example, having a long-term pricing policy with a customer for a set period of time will encourage a long-term relationship, supporting corporate growth for both company and customer. If a company invests in qualifications for Accounts Receivable staff, who can then undertake efficient and effective credit control, they will improve the future earnings and social well-being of that individual. Finally, a tendering policy for capital equipment could only consider suppliers who undertaken sustainable production practices, and enforce strong environmental policies, to support these goals.

Chapter Summary

- Businesses require effective accounting systems to ensure that transactions they enter into are all recorded accurately, are for the use of the business, recorded in the right account and period.
- All effective systems have internal controls which operate to prevent and detect fraud and errors.
- Internal controls include organisation, segregation, authorisation, physical, supervision, personnel, arithmetical and accounting, and management controls.
- The main accounting systems in a business are purchases and cash payments, sales and cash receipts, payroll, inventory and capital expenditure.
- Each system will produce different information and have specific controls within it to ensure the company is run effectively and the systems produce prompt, reliable, accurate and complete information.
- Integrated systems are useful as the risk of fraud or error is minimised – the data is only input once and several postings will be made automatically.
- Integrated systems allow a company to produce and analyse up-to-date information quickly and in sufficient detail to allow them to manage a company effectively. This includes creating information for stakeholders such as customers, suppliers and employees.
- Effective systems can support ethical and sustainable practice by building in suitable controls and procedures to support them.

Key Terms

effective system	a system that records all transactions accurately and reliably
control objective	a statement that addresses how an organisation will manage a risk to it
integrated system	an accounting system where systems such as the sales and purchases ledgers and payroll automatically update the general ledger
internal control	a process put in place by management to prevent or detect fraud or errors eg authorisation, segregation
segregation	the separation of the responsibility for the recording of a financial transaction (eg a sale) and the responsibility for the recording of its settlement (ie the customer paying)
physical control	the use of physical security to prevent fraud, such as a safe or locked cupboard or drawer
inventory count	a comparison between the physical inventory a business holds and its inventory management systems and accounting records

Activities

6.1 You have been asked to set up a 10-character password for Design for Life Ltd's payroll system. Which **one** of the following is the most secure?

(a)	1march1976	
(b)	Two*Nine-7	✓
(c)	0987654321	
(d)	password16	

6.2 You are the Financial Controller of a chain of travel agents and are training a new Accounts Payable Clerk on the reconciliation of the purchases ledger to the purchases ledger control account, a key internal control. The Accounts Payable Clerk asks you 'By doing this does this mean that there will be no problems or errors on the trade payables ledger?'

Explain whether the Accounts Payable Clerk's comment is correct or not, giving examples to support your case.   Not   correct

6.3 You have been asked to specify a new sales system for Trampolines For Fun Limited. Give examples of the types of controls you would look to include in the system for:

- receiving the order and granting credit to customers
- despatching the goods
- raising the invoice
- recording the transaction in the accounts
- receiving payment

6.4 You are S. Poak, the Accountant for Pedal for Miles Limited, a company making bicycles, which employs 60 staff. The payroll bureau that currently manages payroll has become increasingly expensive, so you have been asked to investigate what the company would need to put in place to allow it to manage its own payroll system.

Write an email setting out the main elements of a payroll system to S. Addle, your Managing Director.

6.5 Set out the key controls you would expect to use when making non-current asset purchases and managing the non-current asset register in a company.

6.6 You are Ann Winterfold and work for Summerland Inks Ltd. You have been asked to write a set of procedures for this year's inventory count, as part of the year-end procedures.

Write an email to the Financial Controller, Hamilton Rorsch, setting out the procedures to be followed by both the staff who are counting and by the finance department, to ensure the inventory count is accurate and inventory will be valued correctly.

6.7 Your colleague, Michel, is studying AAT, and is finding it difficult to understand which controls are suitable for certain weaknesses. He has asked you to help him match suitable controls with the following weaknesses.

Select which control is suitable for each of the following weaknesses.

Select from: Segregation of duties, physical access controls, authorisation and approval, competent personnel, check arithmetical accuracy, management controls

(a)	Customer invoices and payments are managed and recorded by the same person	*Segregation*
(b)	Theft of petty cash left on the cashier's desk	*physical*
(c)	There is no detailed variance analysis of expenses, comparing budgeted spend to actual spend	*Management*
(d)	Any staff member can place an order with a supplier	*authorisation*
(e)	A supplier invoice included the wrong amount of VAT	*arithmetical accuracy*
(f)	Staff have been taxed incorrectly on their wages	*competent personnel*

7 Evaluation and review of accounting systems

this chapter covers...

In this chapter we will consider how effective systems can support ethical and sustainable practices. We look at the issues involved in evaluating and reviewing accounting systems.

The review will involve assessing the strengths of accounting systems:

- *seeing how the underlying procedures fulfil the needs of the organisation and its operation*

- *seeing how effective the internal control system is in terms of procedures*

The review will then assess the weaknesses of accounting systems, analysing:

- *weaknesses in accounting systems and company procedures*

- *the possibilities for error and fraud involving the loss of money, inventory and reputation*

- *ways in which sustainable development policies and ethical procedures are supported by the company's procedures*

We will look at how these weaknesses impact on the company, including:

- *cost, reliability and timeliness*

- *time, money and reputation*

Finally, we will consider how a SWOT analysis and PESTLE analysis can help us evaluate the internal controls in an accounting system.

REVIEWING THE ACCOUNTING SYSTEM AND UNDERLYING PROCEDURES

As each organisation grows and changes, different accounting systems and policies will be implemented or discarded. When a small business is set up, the accounting systems may be quite basic and only have limited controls. This is because the accounts are prepared by few people and a small number of people are involved in decision making, so there is no need for systems to be complex.

As a business grows and employs more people, produces more products and sells more goods, the accounting systems it needs will be different. The business may have several members of accounts staff, not just one or two, so the systems in place and the information being generated will be significant in volume and likely to be complex, with different departments requesting information. And so, to ensure a particular accounting system is 'fit for purpose', it will need to be regularly reviewed.

As part of the assessment, you will be asked to review the adequacy of one or more accounting systems. This will be for an organisation in the scenario and reference material, so you will have some prior knowledge of its structure. The review could cover the following areas:

■ The accounting records and financial reporting information: are they sufficient and do they provide the necessary information the company and stakeholders need?

■ The internal control systems: how efficient are they in terms of detecting errors and preventing fraud and do they support ethical standards and sustainable practices?

■ Methods of working: do current practices support the business and its future? Are the computer systems in place to meet the information needs of the company? Are the procedures and processes fit for purpose?

To allow you to review any system thoroughly, you will need to assess the **strengths** of the existing system – in terms of its controls and procedures. You will then need to analyse the **weaknesses** of the system. This is applying the first part of **SWOT analysis,** where the business focuses on the **internal** strengths and weaknesses of an accounting system. We will look at a complete SWOT analysis at the end of Chapter 8, as this will include potential **opportunities** and **threats** as well.

IDENTIFYING THE STRENGTHS OF THE SYSTEM

There are various areas of investigation which will indicate how effective the accounting system is in preventing errors and detecting and deterring fraud.

Using the scenario and reference material given, you could:

- draw up an organisational chart of the accounting system

For a specific accounting system, you could:

- draw a plan of the system, noting who completes which activities and the controls over each step, similar to the system diagrams in the previous chapter
- identify the other operational areas of the organisation which the accounting system supports

You can consider areas which relate to a number of different aspects of internal control by asking a number of questions:

operating procedures, reliability and efficiency?

'Is there a Policies and Procedures (or similar) document?'

'Is the authorisation system for payments clear and workable?'

'Are there the necessary routine checking procedures in place?'

'Are there random checks made to ensure procedures are being followed correctly?'

'Are passwords (both to computers and premises) kept secure and changed when necessary?'

'Are items such as the petty cash box and the company cheque books kept under lock and key and are the keys kept only by authorised staff?'

'Are the reporting lines within the organisation working efficiently?'

'Is the system cost-effective – does it use resources efficiently?'

'Does the system support sustainable practices, eg suppliers who have sustainable policies, sourcing goods locally?'

'Is it easy for customers to place orders?'

'Are there safeguards to ensure ethical behaviour, eg confidentiality guidelines?'

'Is the system completely reliable, eg if staff are away?'

So where the answer to the question above is 'yes' then we can state the system is a strong effective system.

computer systems

The computer system should be integrated, so that all the ledgers automatically update the general ledger, using software such as Sage or Microsoft Office. There should also be IT authorisation controls in place, so that users can only access the parts of the system they need to use in their job. This keeps the data protected and, ultimately, reliable.

By having an integrated system, the business should be able to generate good quality information as and when it is needed. A good computerised system will support the business, so the reports it generates will provide relevant information in a format the managers need and understand. For example, a good system will allow the Financial Controller to produce a statement of profit or loss, to meet financial reporting requirements, as well as the information needed to run and manage the business, such as:

- revenue and costs by product line or location
- labour costs broken down by department, split into indirect and direct costs
- variance analysis for materials and labour costs by product or job
- expenses by type and location
- management accounts in any format the organisation wishes
- customer statements

Obviously this is not an exhaustive list. When evaluating the system, you need to consider the type of business and decide whether the computerised system meets the organisation's information needs or not.

IDENTIFYING THE WEAKNESSES OF THE SYSTEM

The weaknesses, or **deficiencies**, in an accounting system often result in **errors** or in **fraud**.

weaknesses and their impact

Weaknesses result from inefficiencies in the internal control system and can cause all sorts of problems, for example:

- an invoice being sent to the wrong customer
- a duplicate invoice being raised
- a discount being incorrectly calculated
- a payment to a supplier being made very late
- an employee being paid the wrong rate of pay
- a customer being sent a formal demand for an overdue account when in fact payment has already been received but entered to the wrong account
- inventory showing as available on the inventory management system when, in fact, it is not, so a customer order cannot be fulfilled

You will doubtless be able to add other examples to this list of unfortunate accidents. What these examples have in common is that they result in some form of loss to the organisation involved:

- **loss of money** – when a payment is made for the wrong amount or a discount is incorrectly calculated
- **loss of time** – when a problem must be sorted out and emails and apologies sent – time is also money, of course

■ **loss of reputation** – when customer expectations are not met and the organisation loses face – and even its customer's business

lack of review of procedures and its impact

When a business does not periodically review and update its methods of working, they may become unreliable, costly to run and delay the production of information. An example of this is set out below.

Case Study

CLEARGLASS WINDOWS LIMITED

situation

A business, ClearGlass Windows Limited, has used Microsoft Excel for the day-to-day management of Accounts Receivable and Accounts Payable for a number of years. The invoices and receipts and payments are then manually entered into a Sales, Purchases and General Ledger, using journals at the end of the month. The monthly management accounts are produced several weeks after month-end.

required

What problems exist in the current system for ClearGlass Windows Limited?

solution

There are several problems with this system:

- Data is entered twice – onto Microsoft Excel and an accounting software package, which takes time and money. This is not cost-effective.
- Manually entering data is likely to lead to errors in the General Ledger, so information will be unreliable.
- Up-to-date information on supplier and customer balances and aged recoverables will not be available. This could lead to inefficient working practices, where customer debts could be chased once paid or supplier payments might be made twice.
- Production of management account information will be slow and it will be unavailable for several weeks.

RISK AND ITS IMPACT

We covered the risk assessment process in detail in Chapter 4. Now we know what an effective system looks like, we can identify if there are risks within the system, ie there are poor internal controls.

Initially, let's remind ourselves of some possible risks:

■ sales orders being accepted when the price is not agreed

■ goods sold being depatched but not invoiced

- customers being uncreditworthy
- orders being placed without an agreed price or order number
- no receipt procedures when goods arrive at the warehouse
- staff being paid for hours not worked
- no reconciliation of cash takings to the till or the bank

Now we must decide what we should do to monitor, review and report on these risks. Let's look at some examples of how we could do this.

monitoring procedures

- compare budgeted and actual spending, inventory levels, sales or cash takings to see if they are as expected
- record the level of unauthorised orders placed or orders for goods for own use
- record the level of missing items
- compare how much inventory we have to the amount we should have, referring to the purchase orders

review procedures

- look at a sample of orders for appropriate authorisation and price (compared to best price paid)
- perform a walk-through test, ie tracing an item from beginning to end in the accounting system to see where controls are weak. For example, tracing a sales order to signed despatch note, sales invoice, sales daybook, receivables ledger, statement and receipt from customer
- match order to invoice and check inconsistencies with supplier
- use internal audit to review controls and see if any needs strengthening

reporting procedures

- use computer software to identify unpriced orders
- produce monthly inventory reports (tables or charts) showing inventory losses
- summarise the level of credit notes issued in a period due to price disagreements with customers
- tabulate the differences between till records and cash banked on a weekly basis

Remember you can use visualisation tools to make the reporting elements understandable to non-finance managers.

FRAUD AND ITS IMPACT

Fraud, another consequence of poor internal controls, is also covered in Chapter 4, and poses a threat of loss:

■ **loss of money** – monetary-based frauds include payables ledger staff paying fictitious suppliers and diverting the money to their own account, or payroll staff using the same principle to send payroll payments to fictitious employees

■ **loss of inventory or revenue** – for example, a case of an employee over-ordering valuable inventory and then stealing it and arranging for its sale at a nearby street market. Or an employee putting cash sales in their own pocket instead of through the till

■ **loss of time** – employees do not work the time recorded on time sheets

There are plenty of other examples of fraud which could occur in every type of accounting system.

fraud and ethical practices

The opportunity for fraud is closely linked to the ethical standards maintained within the organisation. As part of establishing weaknesses, you will need to look at if there are opportunities for fraud, where controls are weak or do not exist and the lack of ethical principles this allows. For example:

■ non-performance of bank reconciliations, which are a key internal control over the cash book and the business's money. They should be performed regularly (weekly or monthly) and any outstanding reconciling items should be followed up. If an employee fails to do this, they will be breaking the fundamental principle of professional competence and due care and any fraud being committed may not be found until much later

■ personal expenses claimed through the business by the Sales Director – if there is no authorisation process in place over the Sales Director's expenses, they could put through costs which are personal, rather than just for the business. If this were the case, they would be breaking the fundamental principle of integrity

As we can see, where weaknesses exist, professional ethics are more likely to be breached, so a strong system of controls will support good ethical practices.

sustainability

Just as weak internal controls will discourage ethical practices, so weak internal controls and procedures in an organisation can discourage sustainable practices too. For example, a lack of selection criteria for suppliers would allow the business to buy from any supplier. Chosen suppliers may not act in a sustainable manner, which could be detrimental to the business, if publicised.

OVERALL SYSTEM EVALUATION

As we considered in the previous chapter, it is crucial to understand what a good system looks like and the controls it should have. Internal controls that are missing from a system you are reviewing will allow mistakes or fraud to occur, so you can use this knowledge to 'spot the difference'. The diagram below summarises this process:

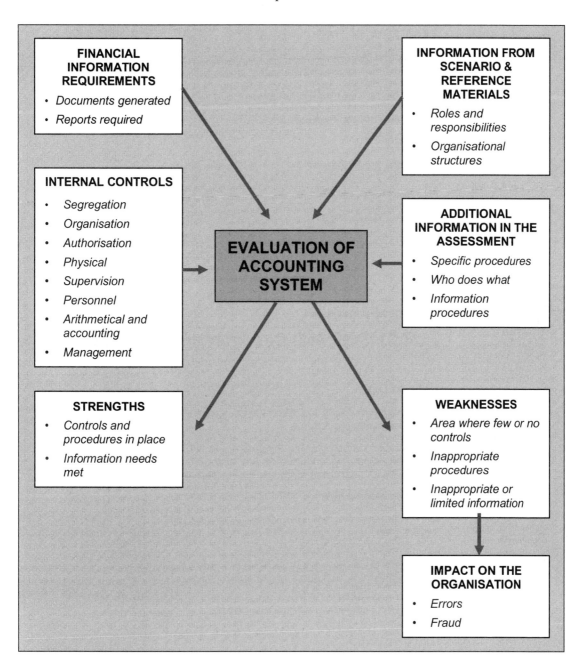

Answering the assessment

In the assessment you will be given detailed information regarding an accounting system. You could then be asked to comment on the weaknesses, or deficiencies, within it and the potential problems or impact on the business because of them.

You may also be asked to consider the causes of the weaknesses, which you have already covered in Chapter 4.

---

examples of weaknesses and the potential impact

You could be asked to review any one of the accounting systems we considered in the previous chapter, namely:

- purchasing and cash payments
- sales and cash receipts
- payroll
- inventory
- expenses
- non-current assets

The following case study indicates the type of information you might be given and the possible weaknesses, causes and potential impact on the organisation.

Case Study

DESIGN FOR LIFE LTD: PURCHASING AND CASH PAYMENT SYSTEM

situation

You have been asked to review the adequacy of the controls in Design for Life Ltd's purchasing procedures.

The company operates an integrated accounting system, which includes a purchase accounting module. Matt Arnold, the Purchasing Manager, is responsible for managing purchasing activities. The system is organised as follows:

Ordering and receipt

All purchases must be documented on a pre-numbered purchase order. Matt Arnold keeps pre-numbered order books and keeps a record of which department the books are issued to.

Orders for production items are signed off by Andrew Roberts, the Warehouse Manager. Capital expenditure is signed off by Aneysha Dickson, the Financial Controller. All other purchase orders can be raised by any departmental budget holder, who approves and signs the order.

The budget holder keeps a copy of the purchase order and sends one to the supplier. The final copy is sent to accounts, for Tina Fay, the Accounts Payable Clerk, to file in the Outstanding orders file. The goods are delivered to the Budget Holder's location and the Budget Holder sends the signed order to Tina.

New suppliers

New suppliers are contacted by Matt Arnold. He provides trade references and requests Credit Terms.

The Finance Director, Joseph Armstrong, sets standard payment terms as 60 days from the end of the month of delivery. If a supplier suggests a prompt payment discount for early settlement, Matt negotiates this independently.

Matt has access to the Supplier Standing Data and enters the supplier's bank information ready for Tina to make payments.

Accounting and paying for purchases

All purchase invoices are sent to Tina Fay. She checks the calculations, matches the invoice to the order held in the Outstanding Orders file and inputs the invoice onto the payables ledger, authorising it for payment.

Tina deals with credit notes and queries with suppliers directly, as and when they arise. All payments are made using BACS. Aneysha Dickson authorises a payment run each week.

required

(a) Identify systemic weaknesses (deficiencies) in the system for purchases outlined above.

(b) Analyse the causes of the weaknesses.

(c) Evaluate the impact that each weakness could have on the company.

solution

(a) Weakness (b) Cause	(c) Impact on company
(a) No evidence of physical inspection of quality and quantity of goods. (b) Lack of formal procedure for receiving goods	Goods could be paid for when they have not been received or are of poor quality or are incomplete.
(a) There are no authorisation limits on purchase orders. (b) Lack of authorisation policy for orders	Large purchases may be made unnecessarily, for a poor price or fraudulently. This could cost the business a lot of money and result in poor cash flow.
(a) Budget holders and Warehouse Manager can both raise orders and receive goods. (b) Lack of segregation of duties	Potential fraud as goods could be taken for own use. Goods that are unnecessary for the business could be ordered.
(a) The supplier terms agreed by Matt Arnold are not approved by the Finance Director (b) Lack of formal procedure for agreeing supplier terms	Potential for fraud by Matt through collusion with suppliers. This would result in higher prices for the company and money paid to Matt.
(a) Tina matches the invoice to the order, not any goods received documents (b) Lack of formal procedures for checking order is received and agrees to purchase invoice	Goods could be paid for, not received.
(a) Aneysha Dickson authorises payment run (b) Lack of formal procedure for authorising BACS payments	Potential theft by Aneysha and Tina through collusion. The BACS payment could be changed to include additional payments.
(a) No authorisation of new accounts (b) Lack of formal procedure for authorising new accounts	Company may not be buying goods at the best price. Potential for theft/ fraud via collusion with suppliers.

Note: We have only considered the weaknesses, their causes and their impact on the company. You are not asked to make recommendations in this question!

As you can see from the above Case Study, you will need to very carefully examine what the business is doing in detail, then compare it to the controls and procedures you know should be in the system.

It is particularly important that you understand what documents are created and what they are used for. Does everyone who needs a copy get one? Are documents matched or reviewed to ensure the information is accurate and for the business only?

You also need to consider who does what to ensure you correctly identify any weaknesses. Are they the right person to do that procedure? Should they have that level of authority?

commercial impact of weaknesses in the business

The potential impacts in the Design For Life Ltd Case Study were simply the errors that can occur and potential fraud. The business and its trade could also suffer due to current procedures – it may not just be confined to the accounting systems, for example:

■ where a business only allows credit applications by post, rather than by email, it could be putting obstacles in the way of trade

■ where a business only trades through shops and has no online sales facility, it may be losing potential customers

Being more aware of the market the business operates in, its competitors and its products is increasingly important for people working in Finance.

We will look at another Case Study now to emphasise this point, using the first part of SWOT analysis. It covers both strengths of current procedures and the benefits to the business, as well as weaknesses and their impact.

Case Study

COOK RIGHT LIMITED: SALES SYSTEM

situation

Cook Right Limited is a small chain of three shops, owned by Paul Goodgrub, specialising in kitchen and cooking equipment. All the shops have been trading for several years.

Sales by shop
Each shop is staffed by a manager and two assistants. The staff have all worked there for several years. Each shop has its own non-digital till, with sales categorised by: baking, electrical equipment, utensils and sundry items.

Every shop has a credit card machine – cash and credit card sales are recorded separately using the till. A till reading is taken at the end of the day and reconciled by the Manager back to the money in the till, allowing for a £100 float. Any differences are recorded on the takings sheet.

The cash is banked every two days, as there are relatively few cash transactions. The cash takings sheets and paying-in slips are posted to the Leeds shop, where the bookkeeper is based. This shop acts as the Head Office.

Internet site
Cook Right Limited has recently set up an internet site to support the three shops. The website shows pictures of a range of current products being stocked. Cook Right Limited does not have a computerised inventory system currently, so no sales are made using the site.

Accounting for sales

The takings sheets and till roll information are used to update the general ledger accounts by the bookkeeper, who totals each category of sale. Sales are then recorded using the shop categories only.

The takings are compared to the bank statements on a monthly basis, when the bank reconciliation is performed. Differences between the takings sheet and the banking or credit card receipts are coded to a suspense account, which is written off to the statement of profit and loss at the end of each year.

The business owner, Paul Goodgrub, reviews the sales information each month and compares it with the previous year's data. Where sales are down, he looks at promotions for the following month to increase sales.

required

(a) Identify the strengths in these procedures for the business. Explain how the business benefits from them.

(b) Identify the weaknesses in these procedures for the business. Explain how these damage the business.

solution

Strengths	Benefits to the business
Takings recorded by sales category	The business can see the type of products customers are buying and can monitor margins earned. This may allow it to improve profitability.
Sales information is produced and Paul Goodgrub reviews it each month, compared with last year. Promotions are set for the following month	Paul Goodgrub is monitoring the level of sales, as the business will need a certain sales level to maintain profitability. Prompt action is taken to drive up sales.
Weaknesses	**Damages the business**
Sales are not recorded in the general ledger by shop	The business cannot determine which shops are selling particular products well so cannot use this more detailed information to improve profitability further.
Non-digital till is being used	Data regarding sales of individual products is not being collected. More targeted promotions cannot be undertaken. Missed opportunity for sales, as they could be higher.
The internet site is not used to make sales	The business is losing out on internet sales and making it hard for customers to buy, as they must go to the shop to do so.
The inventory system is not computerised	The business may be buying inventory in for one shop when it is available to transfer from another. Impulse sales may be lost, if inventory is not in the location the customer is.
	Inventory and margins values can only be determined by an inventory count and valuation. Products that are of low profit or that are unprofitable may be held as inventory ahead of more profitable ones.

PESTLE ANALYSIS

A useful analytical model is **PESTLE analysis**, which focuses on six external factors and the impact on an organisation. The Level 3 Business Awareness unit introduced this model, to help analyse the external environment, so you should be familiar with it. The six factors to consider are:

P	Political
E	Economic
S	Social
T	Technological
L	Legal
E	Environmental

We will now cover these factors in more detail, along with some examples of how they apply to an accounting system.

political factors

Government policies and decision making may affect the way a business operates. Taxation policy, such as higher VAT on particular products, or increasing payroll taxes, such as employers' National Insurance, may reduce the profitability of a business. It will also mean system changes must be made, to make sure the business complies with new regulations and legislation.

The amount of public spending, as well as import and export tariffs, may influence demand for products. When free hot school meals were introduced into the UK for all children under a certain age, catering businesses who agreed to provide them benefitted from an increase in demand. Smaller catering businesses may have needed to invest in better accounting systems to ensure they are paid correctly and on time by the schools.

economic factors

Inflation, interest rates and exchange rates can all reduce or increase the demand for products for a business, as well as increase or decrease the costs of making them.

Where costs of raw materials are rising, due to exchange rates worsening, a business may choose to review its purchasing system, to ensure it always buys at the best possible price from approved suppliers, maximising discounts. This will keep its products competitive, as prices will be kept as low as possible.

social factors

Social factors can also influence how a business operates. These include the amount of disposable income people have, the educational achievement of the local population, demographic changes (for example, changes in size or age of the population) and trends.

A business providing mobility aids to the elderly may experience an increase in direct sales to individual customers, shifting away from supplying local mobility shops, who traded regularly with it and have credit. This change may require the business to improve procedures around collecting payment prior to despatching the goods, as direct customers may only use the business once. It may not be easy to collect payment from direct customers if they have received the goods.

technological factors

Changing technology can be positive and negative for a business. Access to customers via a website can increase market share; using cloud accounting systems can improve efficiency and reduce staff costs, allowing staff to work from home.

However, as technology changes quickly, products and accounting systems could become obsolete, requiring upgrades or replacement. Automation of the accounting system may lead to redundancies, which will unsettle staff and reduce motivation.

legal factors

Any business must comply with the legislation and regulations of the countries it operates in, or risk fines or even risk being shut down. This includes employment laws, such as minimum wage regulations and the Data Protection Act 2018.

A business may have to change accounting systems when the current system does not enable it to comply with these laws easily. For example, where a large business pays employees based on piecework, it still has to ensure employees earn minimum wage, so it may require automatic checks within the payroll system to ensure this happens.

environmental factors

The need to be aware of the impact on a business of environmental change is increasingly important. Consumers are also more aware of whether products are sustainably produced and the reputation of the business can be damaged if customers discover a business acted in an unsustainable way. In recent years, there have been several examples of fashion retailers using suppliers who pay poor wages to employees making the clothes. The publicity has adversely affected the businesses' reputation and, consequently, sales.

An accounting system that uses only approved suppliers, who provide sustainably produced materials, will ensure the business acts sustainably and protects its reputation.

solving the problems

It is important to realise that where problems exist, the company must then design appropriate procedures to deal with them, whilst still delivering accounting system requirements. This will be considered in detail in Chapter 8.

Chapter Summary

- Accounting systems change as businesses grow and adapt. Small businesses will have relatively simple accounting systems and controls, where larger companies will have more complex systems and controls.

- As a business changes, the systems will need to be reviewed periodically to ensure they are 'fit for purpose'.

- Where procedures are not reviewed periodically, this may lead to them being inefficient, not cost-effective and result in delays to produce necessary information for the business.

- Weaknesses in the controls and procedures could lead to errors, resulting in lost time, money or reputation.

- Weaknesses in the controls and procedures could lead to fraud, resulting in lost assets, such as inventory or money.

- Ethical standards can be supported by designing procedures to incorporate them, such as authorisation processes for expenses.

- Sustainable practices can be supported by designing procedures to include them, such as a policy stating the business can only use suppliers who produce products in a sustainable way.

<table>
<tr><td rowspan="7">**Key
Terms**</td><td>**procedure**</td><td>operating instruction followed by the staff, set out by the organisation eg assessing credit limits for new customers</td></tr>
<tr><td>**internal control**</td><td>activity which prevents or detects errors or omissions occurring in the accounting systems of a business</td></tr>
<tr><td>**integrated accounting system**</td><td>a computerised accounting system where the sales ledger, purchases ledger and cash book automatically update the general ledger</td></tr>
<tr><td>**strength**</td><td>a procedure or activity the business does which benefits the business</td></tr>
<tr><td>**weakness**</td><td>an area where the business can improve its performance or operation</td></tr>
<tr><td>**fraud**</td><td>the use of deception with the intention of obtaining an advantage, avoiding an obligation or causing loss to someone else or to an organisation</td></tr>
<tr><td>**PESTLE**</td><td>a method of analysing six factors affecting a business: political, economic, social, technological, legal and environmental</td></tr>
</table>

Activities

7.1 Speedy Car Services Limited fits tyres, brakes, batteries and exhausts at 15 branches around the Midlands. The company employs 70 weekly paid staff and 20 salaried staff, who are paid monthly. It has recently, at its Head Office in Walsall, documented its weekly payroll system, set out below:

Weekly pay

- Weekly paid staff individually complete a timesheet. These are collected together, scanned and emailed to Head Office on a Saturday night by the Branch Manager.

- The Branch Manager completes details of any new starters on a 'Start form'. If the new staff member has a P45, it is attached, along with the employee's bank details. The Branch Manager completes the employment contract. He then sends all of this to HR at Head Office. HR informs the Payroll Clerk.

- The Branch Manager completes a 'Leaver's form' when a staff member leaves and sends it to HR. HR informs Carena Addision, the Payroll Clerk.

- Wages are paid weekly in arrears. Carena inputs the timesheets onto the payroll system.

- Any amendments to standing data are made by Carena. Starters and leavers are amended using the forms sent by the Branch, held by HR.

- The payroll is produced, detailing net pay, deductions and HMRC payments. This is used by Carena to create a cash request.

- Ali Berg, the Assistant Accountant, reviews the payroll and cash request and collects the cash from the bank first thing Thursday morning. Carena makes up the pay packets, including payslips during that day. The cash is sent by courier to the 15 branches late on Thursday to the Branch Manager.

- The Branch Managers distribute the pay packets during Friday to their staff.

Salaries

- Salaried staff are paid monthly by BACS. The payroll is produced by Carena, who also prepares the BACS transfer. The Finance Director authorises the transfer.

- The Finance Director, Rosie Davis, uses Start and Leave forms to authorise starters and leavers, which she gives to HR and Carena.

- Any changes to salaries are authorised by Rosie, using an Amendment to Salary form, which she also gives to HR and Carena.

- All statutory deductions are paid by Ali.

Required:

(a) Analyse the potential deficiencies in the company's internal controls for payroll

(b) Analyse the cause of the potential deficiencies

(c) Analyse the impact of the potential deficiencies

7.2 Ashfords Limited hires coaches to businesses and individuals all over the Midlands and North West. It owns a fleet of one hundred and fifty coaches and renews at least twenty of them every year. It has recently employed a new Finance Director, Julie Bourne, who is keen to ensure capital items are purchased and controlled as efficiently as possible. The following procedures are currently in place for the purchasing of coaches:

Purchase of coaches

The Maintenance Depot Manager, Keith Wrench, can request to purchase a new coach, when he feels the costs of repairing a vehicle are becoming too high. The business has purchased coaches from the same supplier, Comfortable Coaches Limited, for ten years. The owner is a close friend of Mr Ashford, the Managing Director.

Keith Wrench signs a purchase order, which states the standard price - 5% lower than the current list price. A copy of the order is sent to the Maintenance Depot, another to Accounts and the original to Comfortable Coaches Limited. Coaches are purchased outright, not leased. A deposit of 50% is made on order, with the balance due seven days after delivery.

The coach is delivered to the Maintenance Depot for testing by Keith Wrench. He will sign for delivery, then inspect the coach to ensure there are no problems with it. Where problems occur, Comfortable Coaches Limited will send the relevant personnel to fix the problem. The pre-numbered Goods Received Note (GRN) and Delivery Note are both sent to Accounts.

Coaches are usually put into service within one week of delivery.

Accounting for coaches

When the Accounts Department receives the order form, it immediately raises a BACS transfer for 50% of the price, which is authorised by the Financial Controller, Penny Williams. This is recorded in the general ledger as a prepayment. The order is filed in the Coaches Deposit file, waiting for delivery.

When the Accounts Department receives the GRN, the Accounts Payable Clerk, Dil Massey, matches it to the purchase order. The invoice is entered onto the Payables Ledger, once the price has been agreed to the order and it has been checked for accuracy. The General Ledger is updated to reflect the new non-current asset.

The coach details are recorded on a coach spreadsheet by Penny, which states the purchase date, supplier, depot location and price. This spreadsheet also contains the depreciation calculations that are used to update the General Ledger, which Penny applies, according to the depreciation policy. The spreadsheet and General Ledger are reconciled periodically.

Matching the order to the GRN allows Dil to authorise the payment to be made. The supplier will automatically be paid as part of the weekly payment run one week later.

Disposals

Keith Wrench is authorised to sell the old coaches. He negotiates the price and emails the Accounts Receivable Clerk, Luke Adley, with the details of the buyer, to enable him to invoice it.

Accounts raise an invoice for the disposal of the coach, according to Keith Wrench's instructions. Terms are strictly 30 days. Ownership information is forwarded once the money has been received. The coach spreadsheet and general ledger are updated accordingly with the disposal.

Required:

Identify the weaknesses in the system and evaluate the impact that each weakness could have on the business.

7.3 First Class Flooring Limited manufactures and sells wooden flooring to independent shops and retailers across the UK. It is based in Woking and employs 150 staff. It produces a range of high quality products using sustainable wood purchased from 30 suppliers across the globe. The company operates an integrated accounting system, which includes a sales module. The Sales Director, Fred Plank, is responsible for a team of four sales staff.

The sales system is explained below:

New customers

- New customers contact First Class Flooring Limited initially via its website or by telephone. They can complete an information request online, which one of the Sales team will use to determine their individual requirements.

- New customers must trade on a cash basis for three months until they are able to set up a credit account.

- The credit assessment process is performed by Alyson Baker, the Credit Controller. A bank reference and two supplier references are requested. Based on this information, Alyson can determine what level of credit to offer.

- Normal credit terms are 30 days from the end of the month. Alyson sends reminder letters out at 10 days overdue and 30 days overdue. Alyson will then telephone and chase debts by letter and email for up to 90 days overdue before a debt collection agency is involved.

Internet site and promotions

- First Class Flooring Limited has invested heavily in its internet site and it is linked to the sales module and inventory system.

- Customers can complete order requests online for items held in inventory, viewing product specifications and prices. The ordering system will automatically check if they are within their credit limit and will accept the order if this is the case.

- Alternatively, for specially made items, they can phone and place the order with one of the sales team, who will review the credit limit for compliance.

- The company emails out promotional offers on standard products each day, with relevant links to the website to all customers. The software it uses reviews items customers have purchased in the last three months and tailors the offer accordingly.

- Over 70% of sales are made to existing customers. All pricing is loaded into the sales ordering system. The Sales Team can give discounts to customers by amending the price on the sales order.

Required:

(a) Identify two key strengths in these procedures. Explain how the business benefits from them.

(b) Identify two key weaknesses in these procedures and explain how they damage the business.

7.4 You work for a small chain of independent pet shops. You have been asked to look at the procedures over the takings for the shops. As part of this process, you have identified the following risks:

- The till is often left unattended while staff help customers decide between different products.

- A code is required for authorising refunds on the credit card machine and the customer has to sign the refund voucher. Sometimes the manager tells members of staff the refund code, when he or she is busy serving other customers.

- The takings are banked every other day. The cash in the till is counted and compared with the till readings, allowing for a float of £200. There are often discrepancies, both under- and over-banking, after sundry expenses such as paying for milk and window cleaning, have been accounted for. These are not investigated.

Identify the risks within the system and suggest how you can monitor, review and report on them.

7.5 You have been working on PESTLE analysis for Best Care For You Ltd, a business providing in-home care for the elderly.

Your colleague, Shanice, is not familiar with PESTLE and has asked you to show which category is appropriate for the statements given below.

Identify the appropriate category for each statement from the PESTLE analysis findings.

	Political	Economic	Social	Technological	Legal	Environmental
Offer incentives for carers to purchase electric vehicles						
Expected wage increases due to a rise in the minimum wage						
Use tracking software to record hours worked and travel time for carers						
Increasing levels of customers requiring service						
Low employment levels in local area making it easy to recruit staff						

7.6   You work in a medium-sized firm of accountants, Taylor, Lowbridge & Co., with six branches across the South West. You provide accountancy, bookkeeping and taxation services to clients who are both self-employed and run small and medium-sized limited companies. You also provide payroll services, via a payroll bureau, for both weekly and monthly paid staff.

Profits have fallen slightly in the last two years. The practice manager, Denise Lockyer, has been asked to research the factors that could have contributed to this fall and that may influence the accounting systems used by the firm, and the services it provides.

Denise has completed her research, the results of which are set out below:

- 60% of clients are now using cloud-based technology to input their day-to-day transactions. Previously, junior staff would input these transactions into an in-house accounting system. These staff must now review the transactions and be familiar with several different cloud-based accounting systems.

- There has been an increase in self-employed clients and new small businesses. A recent recession led the government offering grants and business support to set-up new businesses. The current in-house accounting package used is proving expensive, as the level of licence required for additional clients has increased.

- Self-employed clients and new businesses are more confident at reading financial information and using the dashboards within the accounting software. It is more difficult for the firm to persuade clients that the information input by them must be reviewed, to ensure it is accurate at all times. This has had a negative impact on client billings for this work.

- Tax laws have become more complicated, making it harder for clients to do their own annual tax reporting. The system used to support tax return submission is cumbersome to use.

- Minimum wage legislation has led to an increase in employers using payroll bureaus. The current software package used has started to charge a cost per employee processed, rather than a one-off system cost. Subsequently, costs to the firm are higher.

- Apprenticeships are now available for AAT students, several of whom are employed by the firm.

- Some staff have been allowed to work from home, as part of an initiative to improve employee engagement. Productivity has fallen slightly.

For each PESTLE category, explain how it has affected the accounting systems and processes of Taylor, Lowbridge & Co.

8 Recommendations and making changes

this chapter covers...

In this chapter we will look at the need to make recommendations for improvements to the accounting system. This includes:

- *identifying suitable changes, whether they are due to organisational requirements or statutory changes*

- *changes that are ethical and sustainable*

- *the costs involved in each recommendation and the likely benefits that will follow*

- *problems that might arise during the transitional period*

- *controls needed in the transitional period while changes are implemented*

- *ways to support staff to adapt to the changes*

- *presenting recommendations to management, including the reasons why an organisation should implement them*

MAKING THE RECOMMENDATIONS

A review of an organisation's accounting system will reveal:

- the **strengths** of its internal control system and its method of operating
- the **weaknesses** of the system and the consequent errors that occur, inefficient procedures and opportunities for fraud
- areas of strength and weakness relating to ethical and sustainability issues

Changes may also be needed as the organisation becomes larger and more complex. For example, imagine a manufacturing company is expanding and setting up a second factory. The site is five miles away from the current factory. New staff and management will be employed to run it. The business will have systems and procedures in place to run a single site, but it will now need to consider issues such as:

- how to collect the information for the new weekly staff, to ensure they are properly paid
- whether to locate accounting staff at one factory or both
- how sales and purchases are going to be recorded at the new site and if the computer systems need to be upgraded to do this efficiently
- how to restructure the general ledger to allow for detailed analysis of both sites

Changes will therefore be made when the current procedures and systems are no longer 'fit for purpose'.

In the assessment, you may need to:

- make recommendations for improvement
- justify those recommendations
- consider any problems that might occur in the transitional period leading up to the implementation of the new systems

IDENTIFYING SUITABLE CHANGES TO THE ACCOUNTING SYSTEM

You could be asked in the synoptic assessment to make changes in an accounting system where there are weaknesses and potential problems. As we explained in Chapter 7, a weakness exists where controls and procedures that should be there are not present. A recommendation must, therefore, solve the problem and stop the weakness by:

- setting out the new procedures or controls which will resolve the issue – this should be detailed enough for a person reading it to fully understand who is doing what and what documents are involved

■ explain the reasons why the business must make the change to the accounting system – this will include benefits to the organisation of making the change. You need to justify to management why the business should be making the change

The Case Study that follows leads on from analysis we did in Chapter 7, where we identified problems with the purchasing and payments system of Design for Life Ltd.

Case Study

DESIGN FOR LIFE LTD: PURCHASING AND CASH PAYMENT SYSTEM

situation

In Chapter 7, on pages 144 to 145 you were asked to review the purchasing system of Design For Life Ltd. You identified the following weaknesses and causes, along with impact on the company resulting from them.

(a) Weakness (b) Cause	(c) Impact on company
(a) No evidence of physical inspection of quality and quantity of goods. (b) Lack of formal procedure for receiving goods	Goods could be paid for when they have not been received or are of poor quality or are incomplete.
(a) There are no authorisation limits on purchase orders. (b) Lack of authorisation policy for orders	Large purchases may be made unnecessarily, for a poor price or fraudulently. This could cost the business a lot of money and result in poor cash flow.
(a) Budget holders and Warehouse Manager can both raise orders and receive goods. (b) Lack of segregation of duties	Potential fraud as goods could be taken for own use. Goods that are unnecessary for the business could be ordered.
(a) The supplier terms agreed by Matt Arnold are not approved by the Finance Director. (b) Lack of formal procedure for agreeing supplier terms	Potential for fraud by Matt through collusion with suppliers. This would result in higher prices for the company and money paid to Matt.
(a) Tina matches the invoice to the order, not any goods received documents. (b) Lack of formal procedures for checking order is received and agrees to purchase invoice	Goods could be paid for, not received.
(a) Aneysha Dickson authorises payment run. (b) Lack of formal procedure for authorising BACS payments	Potential theft by Aneysha and Tina through collusion. The BACS payment could be changed to include additional payments.
(a) No authorisation of new accounts. (b) Lack of formal procedure for authorising new accounts	Company may not be buying goods at the best price. Potential for theft/ fraud via collusion with suppliers.

required

Recommend suitable changes to be made to the accounting system to resolve each of the weaknesses. Explain the benefit for each recommendation, including any assumptions you make.

solution

Recommendation	Benefit and assumptions
Produce a written Goods Received Procedure, which includes inspecting the goods, comparing it to the order and signing the Delivery Note and Goods Received Note (GRN) as proof of the check, noting where anything is damaged or short-ordered, prior to the GRN being sent to Accounts. Only authorised staff should receive goods. Train all staff in this procedure.	Goods will only be paid for if they have been received in good condition and complete. Assume staff will continue to match GRN and the order correctly.
Orders should be authorised by two people, one of whom is a senior member of staff eg a Director.	Staff will be unable to order goods for their own use and receive them when they come in. Purchases information in the financial statements will only include items purchased for the business. The risk of potential fraud will be reduced.
Two people must authorise an order (as above).	Goods will only be purchased for the business at an agreed price. The potential for fraud through collusion with suppliers is removed.
Where payment terms differ to those set as required by the Finance Director, they must be approved by the Finance Director prior to being agreed with the supplier.	The Finance Director will be aware of suppliers where different credit terms need to be met. The Finance Director will be able to monitor and budget cash flow more efficiently. The potential for fraud through collusion with suppliers is reduced.
All invoices must be matched to both the order and the GRN prior to being input onto the payables ledger.	Only items received will be paid for.
Orders must be authorised by two people, one of whom is a senior manager or Director.	Large purchases will not be made unnecessarily, for a poor price or fraudulently. The profitability of the business will be maintained.
Two people need to authorise the payment run, including one Director. There must be supporting documentation with payments.	The business will not make payments unnecessarily. The potential for fraud is reduced. Assume the supporting documentation will be reviewed when the payment run is authorised.
All new accounts should be authorised by the Production Director.	The company will be buying goods at the best price. The potential for fraud through collusion with suppliers is removed.

The recommendations can be beneficial for a number of reasons including:

- they reduce the likelihood of fraud or error occurring
- they make the process more efficient, resulting in time or cost savings
- they will improve customer service and therefore improve the reputation of the business

THE IMPACT OF CHANGES ON OPERATING PROCEDURES

Many of the changes suggested in the purchases system for Design For Life Ltd would have cost little to implement and would have had a relatively small impact on the day-to-day operations.

One area which would have changed significantly was the new Goods Received Procedure. To be effective, it would have to be clearly written and staff would need to be thoroughly trained, especially in procedures when goods are damaged or incomplete. The time taken to receive goods would increase considerably.

Sometimes, one recommended change can have an impact across much of an organisation. The following example illustrates where a change in one area can have implications for almost all the organisation.

Case Study

COOK RIGHT LIMITED: CHANGE TO TILL SYSTEM

situation

The business, Cook Right Limited, has a chain of three shops, specialising in selling kitchen equipment, all of which have been trading for several years. Each shop is staffed by three people who have been employed for several years. The current systems are in place:

- The sales recording is by a non-digital till in each shop and the sales are recorded and categorised by baking, electrical equipment, utensils and sundry items.

- The shops can take payment by cash, debit card and credit card.

- Cash takings are recorded daily on a takings sheet by the Shop Manager. The cash and credit card payments are reconciled at the end of the day to the till roll. Differences are noted on a takings sheet.

- The takings sheets and paying in slips are posted to the Leeds shop, which acts as a Head Office.

- Sales are recorded by category in the general ledger. The bookkeeper adds all the takings sheets together and records each category in total, not by shop. The bookkeeper therefore enters the cash and credit card information manually into the general ledger.

- Currently there is no computerised inventory system.

- Paul Goodgrub, the owner, reviews sales information each month and compares it with the previous year's data. Where sales in a category are down, he proposes promotions for the following month to boost sales.

required

The owner Paul Goodgrub is considering updating the tills in all three shops. Recommend how he could update the system to improve sales and reporting information. State the benefits of the new system and any assumptions you make.

solution

Recommendation

Paul Goodgrub could invest in an Electronic Point of Sales system (EPOS) for each of the three shops.

The benefits of the system would be:

*   Accurate product-by-product sales data by shop, which could automatically update the general ledger at the end of the day.

*   Potential to computerise inventory, allowing accurate profit margin analysis on a product-by-product basis. This would also mean better inventory control and ordering across the shops.

*   More focused promotions on products to increase sales.

*   Quicker identification of slow-moving items and ability to take appropriate action.

*   Paul Goodgrub can have access to accurate sales information in 'real time' without delay due to waiting for takings sheets to be sent through.

Assumptions

*   Cost of EPOS system is acceptable to Paul Goodgrub compared with the benefits it brings.

*   Staff are willing to be trained on a more complex system and will enter the data correctly. The training cost will need to be paid.

*   Bookkeeper can be adequately trained to ensure the data from the EPOS system reconciles back to the takings accurately and reliably. There may be an initial cost.

*   General ledger can be set up to include more complex reporting data. If not, the business may need to reconfigure its general ledger. There will be associated costs.

*   All management reporting will need to be set up for the new data. There will be associated costs.

*   EPOS software can be integrated with the general ledger.

conclusion

The new till system is not simply a different way of recording the data. The operating procedures for staff and the bookkeeper will all change significantly and it will take time to implement. Management always need to consider how cost effective the changes being suggested are – do the costs outweigh the benefit?

HOW MUCH WILL IT ALL COST?

Where any changes are required, the organisation will inevitably incur additional costs. For example, extra costs may be incurred in employing more staff, training staff or acquiring new computer systems. An example cost analysis is shown below.

cost analysis – a practical example

Installation of a sales ordering system	
An estimate of the likely costs is as follows:	
	£
– the cost of the hardware	30,000
– the cost of the software	25,000
– the installation cost	12,500
– the cost of training the staff (see next table)	5,630
– annual maintenance & license fee	6,000
	79,130

When working out a statement of costs you will need to include the **training costs**. These costs include the cost of the time spent training by the employees of the organisation which would otherwise have been spent in productive work. A typical calculation for an organisation might look like the one below. The key point to note is how much each training element costs and how many staff need the training.

time spent by a manager in training	£
20 hours x £50 per hour	1,000
plus 15% on employer costs	
(National Insurance etc)	150
time spent by 8 sales staff in training	
20 hours x 8 x £20 per hour	3,200
plus 15% on employer costs	
(National Insurance etc)	480
time spent by external trainer	
20 hours x £40 per hour	800
TOTAL TRAINING COST	5,630

Sometimes costs, such as market research, are incurred at the start of a project, before a decision is made on the exact system to perform the cost-benefit on. In this case, the costs have been spent, so are not relevant to whether or not to implement the chosen system. These *irrelevant* costs would not be included in the cost calculation on the previous page.

cost-benefit analysis

Cost-benefit analysis compares the amount of resources used (which are measured in money terms) with the benefits obtained from a project (which are not always measurable in money terms).

We have already considered the cost of a new sales ordering system on the previous page.

On the 'benefit' side you will need to analyse the benefits from a project that cannot be measured in financial terms, for example:

■ better communication links between staff

■ an improvement in the quality of a service provided to clients/customers

■ a more effective reporting system

Cost-benefit analysis tells you whether the benefits will outweigh the costs.

assessing the benefits

You may well ask 'How can these costs benefit the organisation?'

Sometimes the benefit will result in cost savings, such as a reduction in inventory holding costs.

A new computerised accounting system means that money savings can be made in the way the system operates, for example:

■ many routine operations will be speeded up which will save time and therefore reduce the wages bill

■ electronic statements of account to customers will save on postage

■ electronic payments to suppliers will also save time and money

■ computer printed invoices will have fewer errors and therefore save time and money

In the assessment, if you are required to cost the savings, or quantify financial benefits, you will be given some information to help you, eg time spent on current procedures. Where you do have to make assumptions, you need to state what they are, eg pay rate, time saved.

cost saving – an example

Cost saving from a new computer system in the Accounts Department	
	£
Time saved inputting data manually from Excel per week	100
(10 hours x £10 per hour plus 15% on employees costs)	15
	115
Yearly saving 52 x £115	5,980

financial benefit

A change to the systems could lead to increased *profits* from additional sales. The benefit would be the additional profit or margin earned, not simply the additional sales, as these sales would only improve cash flow.

financial benefit – an example

Additional sales of products due to an improved website	
	£
Additional sales of £125,000 @ margin of 20% per month	25,000
Yearly saving 12 x £25,000	300,000

Financial benefits would reduce the cost of the change, possibly, but not necessarily, resulting in an overall net financial benefit.

non-financial benefits

There are also benefits which cannot be quantified in terms of money:

- the organisation will appear more professional
- the service provided by the organisation will be more efficient, which means that there will be fewer errors and problems, all of which cost time and money

It is important to consider these non-financial benefits as part of the cost-benefit analysis.

conclusion

In conclusion, you will see that the benefits which emerge from a cost-benefit analysis cannot always be given a monetary value. The final decision must rest on the evidence of all the benefits provided – in basic terms "will it significantly improve the accounting system and is it worth all the money?"

OTHER CONSIDERATIONS

ethical principles

When you are making recommendations, you always need to consider the ethical implications of your suggestions. As a member of the AAT you are bound by the AAT Code of Ethics. Therefore, you need to consider how the recommendations you make in the assessment support the following ethics, which have been considered previously in Chapters 3 and 6:

- objectivity
- professional behaviour
- professional competence and due care
- integrity
- confidentiality

For example:

- **objectivity** – paying staff in the same job a different wage, depending on if you are friends with them
- **professional behaviour** – using abusive language in emails
- **professional competence and due care** – rushing a management report and not checking it thoroughly, as you want to go on holiday
- **integrity** – informing your manager you have completed a job when you have not
- **confidentiality** – telling a customer the profit being made on their jobs

It is good practice to evaluate recommendations against ethical principles to ensure they are supported.

sustainable principles

Where possible, recommendations should also support one or more of the three sustainable principles:

- **corporate issues** – increasing long-term company profits to benefit employees by using fair pricing policies or pricing agreements with preferred suppliers

■ **environmental issues** – conserving the environment and resources by moving to a paperless integrated purchasing system will reduce paper use

■ **social issues** – considering the social well-being of people locally and worldwide, by employing apprentices and training staff in suitable qualifications to benefit the organisations and the individuals

---

Answering the assessment

When asked to offer recommendations, you may not specifically be asked in the requirement to consider ethical and sustainable issues. However, you should include them, particularly when asked to justify why the recommendation should be made.

SWOT ANALYSIS

A useful analytical tool to help bring together the analysis of the current system and what a business could do in the future is a SWOT analysis, where the organisation analyses its Strengths, Weaknesses, Opportunities and Threats for a particular situation or system. We will now look at each of these areas in turn.

Strengths

These are the areas in the organisation where it is currently operating effectively and efficiently and where it is already good at what it does. This could be internal or seen from the point of suppliers or customers. Examples of the kind of areas that you could consider as strengths are:

■ good procedures controlling particular parts of the business eg excellent credit control

■ the service suppliers receive – eg prompt, accurate payment

■ capable, qualified people

■ efficient goods despatch procedures so the correct goods are sent to the customer

■ IT systems and procedures which meet the needs of the business and ensure the quality and timeliness of data

■ strong ethical and sustainable practices supported by management

Weaknesses

These are areas of the organisation or activities where the level of achievement is low. These could be apparent from within the business or be made known from the opinions of customers, employees or suppliers. You have examined weaknesses in systems in Chapter 7. The SWOT analysis can highlight these weaknesses:

- a poor sales system, where customers are chased for payment for invoices they have already paid

- unqualified or inadequate personnel to process information, leading to errors in reporting and decision making data

- a non-integrated accounting system

- an inadequate system for recording cash sales

- an ineffective internet site, which customers cannot easily navigate – this will not encourage them to make purchases

- inadequate or inappropriate sales ordering processes

Essentially you are looking for areas the organisation can improve.

Opportunities

The business should consider how it can improve its internal controls and operating procedures, considering external factors, such as those considered in the PESTLE analysis in Chapter 7. Again, this could benefit customers or suppliers. Examples include:

- installing new IT systems, to integrate online websites, inventory management systems and sales ordering and make reporting more timely

- implementing a paperless purchasing system, to provide a more efficient service to suppliers

- implementing new electronic sales initiatives to improve customer service and sales, and reduce marketing cost

- developing new products that can appeal to growing sections of the population, such as the elderly

- investing in new machinery, when interest rates are low and the cost of capital is cheap

Threats

Finally, threats are obstacles the business faces in its current environment and PESTLE can help identify these. Threats could arise for many different reasons – for example, potential problems with customers or competitors. They could also arise through changes in technology or the environment in which the business operates. Examples include:

- competitors launching new and more attractive products

- over-reliance on individual customers or specific contracts

- changes in technology making it harder to compete

- demand in the market for the products of the business

- over-reliance on specialist suppliers

- the pace of change in the market

HOW CHANGE AFFECTS STAFF WHO USE THE SYSTEMS

supporting staff through changes in accounting systems

Any significant change in the accounting system will clearly impact on the staff involved. They will feel challenged, and perhaps threatened.

Part of any recommendation for change should include a plan for ensuring that the staff will acquire the necessary skills and knowledge so that they can use the revised system effectively – for example, where a new or updated computer system is recommended. This could include:

- internal training courses and external training courses
- 'teach-yourself' facilities such as manuals, DVDs, online tutorials and the 'Help' menus provided with the computer software
- telephone support lines made available by the software provider (Sage, for example, provide an excellent 'helpline')

Staff training can be an expensive item and should form a prominent element in the cost-benefit analysis which assesses the total costs of a recommendation against the benefits provided.

changes to organisational procedures

Recommendations may include other modifications to the internal control system which will impact on staff because they will change everyday procedures. For example:

- improvements to credit control procedures, eg credit references on new customers
- improvements to payment procedures, eg sending of BACS payments and Faster Payments to suppliers
- increased security of cash handling, eg having two people to check tills
- increased password security, eg changing passwords regularly
- stricter procedures relating to confidentiality (a fundamental ethical principle)

These changes would need to be communicated to staff, incorporated in the procedures of the accounting system, and monitored on a regular basis.

changes to external regulations

Changes to external regulations may also mean that the staff need to amend working practices, to ensure they continue to comply with the statutory regulations, ie legislation and also the accounting standards. Examples include:

- Taxation regulations affecting areas such as:

  – PAYE for individuals on payroll, Income Tax, National Insurance and other deductions. When real time reporting was introduced by HMRC, payroll staff needed to ensure payroll was being produced accurately and promptly enough to allow them to comply. This will have changed the collection and processing of data in many organisations.

  – VAT – if VAT rates change for certain types of items, such as energy costs or hospitality, the accounting staff may need to review the methods of coding and processing purchase invoices, to ensure the new correct amount of VAT is claimed back. There may also need to be amendments to the standing data for these suppliers and a new VAT rate set up on the accounting system.

- Company law – set out in the Companies Act 2006 – requires that company financial statements (of larger companies) should be audited; these statements are drawn up in a set format and sent to shareholders. Where the format of the accounts is changed or updated, the organisation will need to review its reporting and accounting practices to ensure the data it collects will enable it to comply with this legislation

- International Accounting Standards – these are often updated to reflect changes in the requirements of users of the accounts. Where changes occur, the staff may need to make changes to the accounts within the general ledger – for example, to collect additional information – so the financial statements can comply with the new International Accounting Standard

- Data protection law – set out in the Data Protection Act 2018 – protects data, including financial data, relating to individual customers. There should be strict policies over the protection of data for payroll, customers and suppliers. Any changes to this law, such as a decrease in the length of time the organisation can keep information for, could mean the payroll, customer and supplier databases would need a review policy put in place

MOVING FROM ONE SYSTEM TO ANOTHER

problems that might occur

Inevitably, there will be a 'transition period' moving from one system of operation to another where employees are familiar with the current methods of working but need to learn and implement the new methods. It may simply be a new credit control policy for new customers, which affects the Credit Controller alone, or it could be the introduction of a completely new integrated computerised accounting system. Whatever the change is, you need to consider the problems that could arise in this transition period.

■ Integrity and capture of data – data could be lost or transferred incorrectly

■ Controls may cease to operate or be less effective – eg credit control may not occur as the staff are busy transferring data, rather than chasing customers for payment

■ The service given to customers and suppliers could be adversely affected – Accounts Receivable may be taking longer to deal with queries if running on two systems temporarily or they could incorrectly chase debts already paid. It is important for all staff to have realistic expectations of what may or may not be achieved during the transition period

■ Staff may be demotivated and unwilling to engage with the changes required for the business, particularly if there are some redundancies. This will make implementing a new system more difficult and possibly take a lot longer than expected

■ Productivity may decline when the system is changed. This may be due to the additional work required during the transition (see below) or due to the staff being demotivated

managing a transition

To ensure the changes are implemented smoothly and the new system works, the organisation could implement the following:

■ **Direct changeover** – this is when the old system is 'turned off' at the end of one day and the new system is 'turned on' at the start of the next day. The new system will be fully tested and ready. The staff must also be fully trained in the new system to use this approach. The information moved over from the old system to the new system will need to be reconciled.

■ **Dual or parallel running** – where a complete system (for example, a new sales ledger) is being installed, the business could input all the data onto both the new and old system for a period of time, to ensure the new system is working correctly. This allows the staff to get used to the new system more slowly. The two systems must be reconciled and any differences investigated and resolved prior to the old system being run down and turned off.

■ **Test databases** – often a business will test new software in the 'test' part of the current system to ensure it works properly. They may input data which tested the controls within it (eg authorisation limits) to see if they work properly. They will then swap systems once they are confident they work as expected and the staff are used to the new system. The information moved over from the old system to the new will need to be reconciled.

■ **Phased implementation** – rather than overwhelm staff with changes, a business could implement them in a phased way, ie one new system or process at a time. For example, rather than implement an entire integrated purchasing system, they could implement purchase ordering, followed by a new purchases ledger, then the new cash payments system. As each system is implemented, the staff and management review it and agree when it is working as it should and they are ready for the next phase. Any data transferred between the old and new will need to be reconciled.

■ **Piloting changes** – to see if the new procedures will work effectively, the business could pilot them in certain areas. Only a small number of staff may be involved initially. If it has several locations or companies, the new procedures could be put in place in one location to see where problems may arise and if the new system is viable. The approach taken can be changed, so any issues are resolved prior to it being 'rolled out' to the rest of the business. For example, a new credit assessment procedure for new customers could be trialled for three months at one organisation to see if it is better than the current procedure. It should be noted that it can temporarily put usual business activities under more pressure.

To ensure the process is properly controlled, the staff must be sufficiently trained prior to the change in the system or procedure, rather than after it. The staff will, no doubt, be worried about working in a different way. By training them beforehand, they will be able to inform management of any areas they believe will be difficult to implement or more costly than management expect. They are also more likely to co-operate if they feel involved in the process at an early stage.

If the system change is significant, the business should consider how to manage any potential impact on customers or suppliers where they could be affected. For example, where a new payments system is being installed, the business may choose to pay some invoices early to minimise any potential impact on the supplier's cash flow. If there were any problems during the implementation, this could lead to delays to payments, and by paying early the business would have more time to resolve the issue.

Answering the assessment

You may be given one area of the accounting system to focus on, such as the sales system. You will be given the current operating procedures, which have weaknesses within them and you may have to consider whether they are commercially damaging to the business and cause problems. Any recommendations you make will need to limit or stop the damage to the business or solve the problem.

Chapter Summary

- An organisation requires the accounting system to change over time as the organisation develops, so all systems should be periodically reviewed to ensure they are 'fit for purpose'.

- Any changes to the system or procedures must be suitable for the organisation in terms of reducing the likelihood of fraud or errors, making the process more efficient or improving the service given and therefore reputation of the business.

- Where recommendations are made, the benefits to the organisation should be explained, as well as the likely costs associated with them and how these are arrived at, so that management can justify the change.

- Any changes are likely to have an impact on the staff in the organisation. They may need additional training and support during this period of change.

- Staff may also need to change accounting systems and working practices when statutory regulations or organisational requirements change.

- Problems may occur as procedures or systems move from an old to a new system. The service to customers and suppliers may be disrupted, staff may find the changeover difficult and demotivating, and the data which is moved across may have errors within it.

- Controls should be put in place to minimise the likelihood of these problems occurring, including staff involvement and training, communication with customers and suppliers, and controls over the transfer of data. New systems should be implemented in a planned manner.

- Where changes are suggested, recommendations should consider their ethical and sustainable impact and support these.

<table>
<tr><td rowspan="6">**Key Terms**</td></tr>
<tr><td>**fit for purpose**</td><td>the system will do the job it was designed to do efficiently</td></tr>
<tr><td>**SWOT analysis**</td><td>an analytical tool to consider the strengths, weakness, opportunities and threats of a business and its procedures</td></tr>
<tr><td>**transition period**</td><td>the period where an organisation moves from an old accounting system, or part of an accounting system, to a new one</td></tr>
<tr><td>**statutory regulations**</td><td>the laws which the organisation must comply with</td></tr>
<tr><td>**cost-benefit analysis**</td><td>the comparison of the amount of monetary resources used with the benefits obtained from a project. Non-financial factors should also be taken into account</td></tr>
</table>

Activities

8.1 The company you work for has grown quickly in the last two years and the finance department has doubled in size.

Complete the following statements regarding its accounting systems and staff:

As the business has experienced rapid growth, the accounting system should be **reviewed / replaced / kept the same** to ensure the reporting information it provides **remains the same for managers / is fit for purpose.**

When new staff are inducted, they should be trained **in the importance of internal controls / to follow current procedures.**

A new bespoke system **would / would not** be a cost-effective way of improving the current system.

8.2 Travel America Limited is a travel agency that arranges holidays in the USA. It has five outlets in locations around the country as well as a call centre in Birmingham. The company specialises in tailor-made holidays for independent travellers. It has experienced tough competition in the last few years as the internet has eroded the lower margin side of its business. It is now focused on customers who travel First or Business Class, who will pay to experience 'unique moments' on their holidays. Many customers are repeat business.

You have been asked to review the purchases system and make recommendations for improvement.

Ordering and booking

Bookings generally consist of flights, accommodation, trips and tours. Every holiday is individually costed using the hotel rates and margin information that is loaded into the contracts side of the Reservations system.

Budgeted US dollar requirements are entered in the accounting system for the year by fixing the currency exchange rate in advance. This protects Travel America Limited from significant exchange rate fluctuations. The exchange rate is set in the system for the year and dollars purchased in advance to set the rate.

The Reservations system automatically emails a request to the hotel for the accommodation. Each day, the Sales Manager of each outlet reviews the email confirmations and gives them to the sales consultant to update the status to 'Confirmed' in the system.

Flights are purchased using an online booking engine. The sales consultant searches and finds a flight, then reserves it for the customer. The airline booking engine automatically updates the cost information in the Reservations system. The Reservations system applies the appropriate margin for that fare to give the customer a price. All flight costs are in Sterling.

Tours are booked on a 'Request basis' using the cost and margin information in the Reservations system via automatic email. They are confirmed in the same way as the hotels.

Customers pay a 10% deposit on booking and the balance is due eight weeks prior to departure from the UK.

Suppliers

Travel America Limited deals with luxury hotels and tours, so it has contracts with most of its suppliers, at fixed hotel rates.

Where a new supplier is required, Travel America Limited will initially request 30 days credit, supplying recent financial information, bank references and references from key suppliers. Often this will secure credit. If not, it will request to pay 10% deposit and full payment on arrival date.

Travel America Limited has contracts with all airlines that fly to the USA. The airline tickets are paid for using the Billing and Settlement Plan system, where airlines submit electronic data by ticket and agent to a centralised agency, which then collects payment from the agent for all the airlines they contract with.

Accounting for and paying for purchases

Costs are held on a booking-by-booking basis within the Reservations system.

The Reservations system has an integrated payables ledger, where all hotel and tour suppliers' accounts are held. Payment terms for each supplier are loaded into the Reservations system. Payments for hotels and tours are made in US dollars, according to credit terms, using the Reservations system. The booking is updated with the payment, and costs correctly updated accordingly.

The Accounts Payable team generates payments and completes the payment run information. A payment run is made each week. The Financial Controller, Dua Phiri, authorises the BACS payment.

Flight payment data is downloaded from the Reservations system and compared with the file of payments due from BSP each month on the first of the month. The BSP payment information is then uploaded back into the payments part of the payables ledger of the Reservations system. BSP is taken automatically seven days after Travel America Limited receives the file, ie 8th of the month. Flights are requested by BSP four weeks prior to travel.

The Reservations system generates a journal each month which states the purchases made, by type – flights, hotels, tours, insurance – and the cash paid. This is used to update the general ledger. The supplier payments are reconciled to the US dollar and UK cash book during the next month.

Required:

You are required to identify four features of these procedures:

- Identify a strength and explain how the business benefits from this.

- Identify a weakness in these procedures. Describe the potential damage this weakness could cause the business and suggest a remedy.

- Identify an opportunity to improve the procedures. Explain how the procedures should be changed and how the business could benefit.

- Identify one threat to the effectiveness of these procedures. Explain how the threat can damage the business and suggest an action that would reduce the risk.

8.3 Best Bathrooms Limited makes and sells baths, sinks and sanitary ware to retailers and online. It has several well established product lines, which it carries in inventory. It has a factory in Cardiff and employs 85 people. It currently deals with 300 regular customers, who account for 70% of its sales. It has been trading for several years.

You have been asked to carry out a review of the sales order processing and despatch procedures and make recommendations for improvement.

You have interviewed the Sales Director (Jacob Dyer), Finance Director (Andy Clarke), Credit Controller (Tracey Misham), Warehouse Manager (Kris Nowak) and Accounts Receivable Clerk (Jayne Grey). Your findings are below:

Sales ordering

- Customers are able to order a current catalogue over the phone or view it as a pdf file online, using the internet site.

- Order forms can be completed online to be processed by the Sales Department.

- Orders are pre-numbered sequential documents.

- The Sales Department will contact the customer within 48 hours to confirm the order, price and delivery date. Sales staff can discount the list price to close the sale.

- The order will be printed off three times. The original order will be emailed back to the customer, Sales retains one copy and one copy goes to Kris Nowak.

New customers

- Retail customers can apply for credit. They must provide two years' accounts, two supplier references and a bank reference. Tracey Misham will use a credit agency and the information provided to set a credit limit, authorised by Andy Clarke.

- Online customers must pay using PayPal or by direct transfer through the bank. Jayne Grey will email the warehouse when payment has been made.

- Credit terms are 30 days and are all authorised by Andy Clarke.

Despatch procedures

- Kris Nowak reviews the outstanding orders file daily to ensure no items are waiting to be despatched for longer than a few days.

- The warehouse staff take the order from the file and 'pick' the items on it from the shelf or location in the warehouse and box them or pallet them ready for despatch.

- A three part pre-numbered Goods Despatched Note (GDN) is generated and signed by the warehouse staff to confirm the condition of the goods. One copy is attached to the order and these are both sent to Accounts, who will use them to raise the invoice. Two are sent with the Delivery Team.

- The customer signs for the goods and keeps one copy of the GDN. The signed copy comes back to Best Bathrooms Limited as proof of delivery and is filed in the 'proof of delivery' file in the Warehouse.

Required:

Make recommendations to the internal controls and procedures of Best Bathroom Limited's sales ordering, new customer and despatch procedures and explain the benefits to the business.

8.4   Regal Hotel Limited owns a chain of hotels in the Cotswolds. It has been trading very successfully for several years. The accounts department is based in Evesham. It employs 70 permanent staff and uses casual staff in the summer months, its peak season, to cope with the additional customers and their needs.   There is an Area Manager, who oversees the Hotel Managers.

You have been asked to review the payroll system and make recommendations for its improvement.

Starters and leavers

- Each hotel manager is authorised to advertise for any staff, including casual, short-term contracted staff, when needed.

- The hotels tend to employ staff who have experience and they are often not from the local area. The turnover of casual staff is very high.

- Weekly paid staff are given contracts that are 'zero–hours' contracts, where shifts are not guaranteed.

- The Manager completes a 'New starter form' and fills out the standard temporary contract, completing the hourly rate as per the Head Office rates schedule. This is based on age and experience.

- The Manager also completes the employee details, including bank details. Both parties sign it.

- The employee must provide evidence of their right to work in the UK.

- All this information is sent to Head Office to verify and input into the payroll system.

- Leavers sign a 'Leavers form', authorised by the Hotel Manager. This is sent to HR, who confirm details to the Payroll Clerk, Mary Billesley.

- The Financial Controller, Tim Coleborne, is informed of all leavers and confirms they have been removed from the payroll.

Weekly and monthly payroll

- All staff have to clock in and clock out, using a swipe card each day. This system records their working hours.

- The Manager is usually there at the start of the shift five days out of seven.

- Where staff work longer than 40 hours per week, they will be paid overtime at basic rate plus a half. During the summer, this frequently happens, as casual staff tend to 'come and go'.

- Mary, who works in the Evesham Head Office, takes the information from the clocking in systems and manually enters each person's hours and overtime into a payroll system. This takes approximately three hours each week. Mary is paid £15 per hour.

- The system calculates appropriate deductions and generates weekly pay slips.

- Mary uses this to generate a weekly BACS request. The BACS request is authorised by the Tim.

- All other staff are paid monthly. The procedures for recruitment are all controlled by HR at Head Office, except for the interview process. The Managing Director, Jake Elmsley, signs off all new monthly paid staff.

- The monthly payroll is processed by Mary and generates the BACS report. The BACS request is authorised by Tim.

Required:

(a)   Identify weaknesses in the procedures within the business, the problems they could cause the organisation and make recommendations to resolve them.

(b)   The business has investigated integrating the payroll system with the clocking in system. The integration software will cost £500. The Financial Controller has asked you to prepare a cost-benefit analysis for the integration. Include non-financial factors to consider. Assume employer costs of 15%.

(c)   Identify the problems that could occur with the change in system and suggest actions you can take to limit them.

8.5   You are helping your Finance Director prepare for implementing a new inventory system.

Identify whether the following characteristics are associated with dual running a new system.

Characteristic	Associated	Not associated
Decreases risk of loss of data		
Speeds up the implementation process		
Low cost		
Increased workload on staff temporarily		

8.6   Beautiful Tableware Ltd has recently been reviewing its accounting systems and completed a cost-benefit analysis. You have been asked to categorise some of the suggested changes for the Board of Directors, into social, corporate and environmental.

Identify the appropriate category for the following statements:

Suggested change	Social	Corporate	Environmental
Install new motion sensitive lighting			
Purchase inventory using 12 months supply contracts, to secure beneficial discounts			
Sponsor local high-achieving employees through local pottery design course			
Invest in new inventory management system to reduce inventory holding levels and warehouse requirements			

8.7 Footy for Fun Ltd manufactures table football games. The custom-made division has been expanding in recent years and is considering upgrading its sales ordering system. You are the Financial Controller.

Currently, the range of finishes available for football tables is restricted. A new supplier, Design & Surfacing Ltd, which offers a much wider range of table finish materials, has suggested linking Footy for Fun Ltd's current sales ordering system to its inventory system. Products could then be costed in 'real time' for customers, with the help of trained sales staff.

Some preliminary work was completed by Footy for Fun Ltd, to determine if this was feasible, costing £2,500. Subsequently, you have been asked to produce a cost-benefit analysis for the project.

Initially, three sales staff need to be trained to produce quotations using the linked systems. This would take two days per sales person and cost £400 per person per day. It will cost £15,000 to link the systems together initially and Design & Surfacing Ltd requires a yearly fee of £5,000 for continued access to its inventory system. Footy for Fun Ltd also requires three new computers, costing £4,500 in total.

A chain of sports bars had recently placed an order for 20 customised football tables, each costing £5,200. Discussions with the managing director of the chain indicate additional orders of £180,000 will be placed, once the new materials are available. A profit margin of 40% is earned on custom-made tables.

(a) Complete a cost-benefit analysis for the above proposal.

Costs	£
Benefits	
(Net cost)/benefit	

(b) Identify **four** non-financial factors that should be considered as part of the cost-benefit analysis.

(c) Recommend, with two reasons, whether the proposed investment should be made.

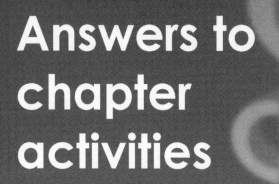

Answers to chapter activities

CHAPTER 2: THE ACCOUNTING FUNCTION – HOW IT WORKS

2.1   (b)   The directors of the company

2.2   **(a)**   False

   (b)   False

   (c)   False

   (d)   True

2.3   **(a)**   Invoicing sales, collecting money from customers, travel expenses, paying staff, room hire, website fees, mobile phones costs.   The main accounting functions would be payroll, sales ledger and purchase ledger.

   (b)   A flat structure. As both owners are involved in the business and it has few employees, you would expect there to be few layers of management within it.   All the recruiters would probably report to one of the owners and there would only be few support staff, the main one being the accountant.

2.4   **(a)**   Invoicing, collecting money from customers, paying staff, costing, paying suppliers and factory overheads.   The main accounting functions would be costing, payroll, purchase ledger, sales ledger and cashier.

   (b)   A hierarchical structure. As the business has two divisions, with many staff, the business would need several layers of management to control production, distribution and selling the products.

2.5   **(a)**   A hierarchical structure.   Due to the size and complexity of the business and its geographical spread, the company will need many different management and employee roles to allow it to operate efficiently, effectively and safely. It will need to have a Board of Directors who are accountable for specific areas, then a team under each of them to deliver in those areas.

   (b)

EMAIL
To: All Payroll staff
From: Charlotte Churchill, Payroll Manager
Cc: Finance Director, Human Resources Manager
Subject: Change in Income Tax rates and treatment of travel discounts
Payroll staff
As you may know, the tax rates on wages and salaries are due to change at the start of the new tax year. The payroll system should automatically be updated for the new rates and personal allowances. However, to ensure it is working correctly, you must manually calculate a sample of net wages calculations and agree it to the system. Any errors must be reported to me immediately.
The rules for travel discounts have also been changed and any member of staff who is given a discount must be taxed accordingly. An additional amount must be calculated reflecting the value of the discount and added to their wages or salary, to be subject to tax as if it were salary.

> **Human Resources**
>
> You need to email to all managers to ensure they inform all staff that the tax rates are changing this month and to contact payroll if they have any queries with their wage deductions. You must also circulate the new rules for taxing discounts given as part of normal pay, to ensure staff are aware of the change.

2.6 **(d)** All of the Directors – The Directors run the business together, so legally they are all responsible if the company does not comply with changes in legislation.

CHAPTER 3: STAKEHOLDERS AND THEIR INFORMATION NEEDS

3.1 **(a)** The bank is a key external stakeholder. The business needs to be able to meet any terms of the loan and also to be able to make repayments and pay the finance charges each year.

The bank may need information such as quarterly management accounts to monitor profitability and cash flow.

The parts supplier is a key external stakeholder. It is important that Speedy Car Services Limited is able to fit whatever a customer requires, as much of the trade is walk in, rather than booked in advance. If the business cannot provide the tyre or part required they are likely to lose the sale.

The supplier is likely to have given credit terms to Speedy Car Services Limited. It will require yearly financial accounts to monitor the business' cash flow and the ability to repay debts on time, as per the agreed credit terms.

The Government is a key stakeholder, as it wants the business to trade and employ staff and pay income taxes, company taxes and VAT.

The Government will want to see the financial statements to determine the profits generated by the business and so its likely tax revenue.

The employees are key internal stakeholders. They have worked for the business for several years and are likely to have pensions through it.

The employees are unlikely to have access to the financial accounts. If they work to bonuses, they are likely to want to see weekly and monthly sales figures to allow them to calculate their bonuses.

The owners are key internal stakeholders. They work in the business and will want it to continue to provide them with a salary and dividends.

(b) The owners are likely to monitor the following:

Performance indicators

- Gross profit margin %, by product and branch
- Operating profit margin % by month

Budgetary control reports

*   Weekly sales figures by branch and product

*   Parts wastage % (Value of wasted parts/ total parts purchased) x 100

*   Labour % (Labour cost as a percentage of sales) x 100

*   Overtime as a % of labour cost

3.2 **(a)** The customers are key stakeholders. The product is very specialised and there are few businesses that supply these products. This is evidenced by the repeat business and long-term nature of the customer relationships.

The customers are likely to want to see the financial statements, to allow them to analyse Almost Vintage Limited's liquidity and gearing, to ensure it will continue to trade and supply them. They may also investigate the gross profit margin, when considering future pricing.

The suppliers are key stakeholders. They want Almost Vintage Limited to continue to trade so they can continue to sell to it.

The suppliers will want to see the financial statements to determine how much credit they should give Almost Vintage Limited.

The owner Narita is a key stakeholder. She will want to know how the business is performing and how profitable it is so she can take money out in the form of salary and dividends.

The employees are key stakeholders. They want Almost Vintage Limited to continue to operate and provide them with stable employment.

The employees will want to see the financial statements to see the business is financially secure and is likely to be able to pay its debts in both the short- and long-term.

(b) The owners are likely to monitor the following performance indicators and include this information on:

Performance indicators

*   Gross profit margin % by product

*   Operating profit margin %

*   Weekly/monthly sales figures

*   Trade receivables collection period (days)

*   Trade payables payment period (days)

Budgetary control reports

*   Labour cost %

*   Wastage % (material wasted/ total material purchased)

*   Overtime % (overtime payments / total wages)

3.3

Ratio	Formulae	Calculation
Gross profit margin	Gross profit / Revenue x 100(%)	15,200 / 36,000 x 100 = 42.2%
Operating profit margin	Operating profit / Revenue x 100(%)	1,890 / 36,000 x 100 = 5.3%
Return on capital employed	Operating profit / (Total equity + Non-current liabilities) x 100(%)	1,890 / (26,950 +3,500) x 100 = 6.2%
Current ratio	Current assets / current liabilities	7,453 / 2,711 = 2.7 : 1
Acid test / Quick ratio	Current assets – Inventories / Current liabilities	7,453 – 2,736 / 2,711 = 1.7 : 1
Gearing	Non-current liabilities / Total equity + Non-current liabilities x 100(%)	3,500 / (26,950 + 3,500) x 100 = 11.5%
Inventory turnover	Cost of sales / Inventories	20,800 / 2,736 = 7.6 times
Inventory holding period	Inventories / Cost of sales x 365	2,736 / 20,800 x 365 = 48.0 days
Trade receivables collection period	Trade receivables / Revenue x 365 (days)	3,960 / 36,000 x 365 = 40.2 days
Trade payables payment period	Trade payables / Cost of Sales x 365 (days)	1,786 / 20,800 x 365 = 31.3 days

3.4 (a) Engaging in unethical behaviour

3.5 (b) Confidentiality

3.6 (c) Social equality

3.7 (a) and (c) improve ethics and sustainability

3.8 **(a)** Not correct

(b) Correct

CHAPTER 4: INTERNAL CONTROL SYSTEMS AND FRAUD

4.1 **(a)**   lack of controls

(b)   poor implementation of controls

(c)   lack of monitoring

(d)   lack of leadership

4.2

Internal control	Purpose	Control suitable - Yes or No?
The Financial Accountant reviews the BACS payment for wages and compares it to payroll, prior to authorising it along with the Financial Director	Prevent and detect fraud	Yes
Two people open the post each day to record customer receipts	Compliance	No*
Monthly backups of data to an offsite server	Safeguard assets	No**

* This control will prevent and detect fraud

** This control will facilitate operations

4.3 The above may result in the occurrence of **theft of cash** fraud that occurs as a result of **lack of controls**. In order to address this fraud risk, Cara and Ben need to implement **a series of physical controls** as soon as possible, to minimise the impact on the **assets**.

4.4

Internal control	Small	Large
Segregation of duties for the posting of sales invoices and credit notes, receiving customer receipts and updating the trade receivables ledger		✓
All payments are authorised by the Managing Director	✓	
Daily bank reconciliations are performed, using automated software		✓

4.5

Improvement	Promote	Not promote
Ensure originals of qualifications for new employees are obtained and copied	✓	
The accounting system requires automatic password changes every 30 days for all staff	✓	
A register of employees who have relationships with staff at customers or suppliers is maintained and regularly reviewed	✓	
A new policy allows finance staff to work from home for up to five days per month, to save them commuter time and travel costs		✓

4.6 (d) All of the above – All the directors are jointly responsible for putting in systems and controls to prevent and detect fraud.

4.7 Misappropriation of assets (theft), misrepresentation of financial statements (false accounting), bribery and corruption, deception.

4.8 Segregation of duties is where no one person is able to completely record a financial transaction from beginning to end.

For example, a person cannot create or raise a sales invoice, then collect and record the receipt from the customer.

This prevents fraud as it would need two or more people to hide or remove the transaction, known as collusion. Two people would need to be dishonest and work together which is less likely than an individual acting alone.

4.9 (a) **Theft of cash sales** – Customers order and pay for one-off items on site and Gino has no record of their 'order'. The invoice book is generic. The gardener could use a similar invoice book he has purchased and give this to the customer, as a receipt. The gardener could then take the money.

Claiming additional hours not worked – The employee could submit additional hours for the maintenance work done, which was not performed, and be paid for this.

(b) *Grading of risk*

Theft of cash sales

Risk of Fraud – High. As employees know there is no system for tracing back missing sales, which could be a reasonable amount at certain times of year, they could easily commit the fraud.

Claiming additional hours not worked

Risk of fraud – High. Employees are aware there is no control over recording how long they spend doing each job.

(c)   *Implications for the business*

Theft of cash sales

Gino would not know of the sale, so will lose sales and profit. The one-off items are likely to be relatively small compared to the day-to-day contracts.

Claiming additional hours not worked

Gino pays the gardeners based on the timesheets, so these additional payments would reduce profits in the business. Gino has knowledge of the business and knows how long it should take for each maintenance job. He would be likely to query additional hours if they were significant.

(d)   *Safeguards to minimise risk*

Theft of cash sales – Customers need to request additional work via email to Gino. He will then be able to match the request to an invoice and payment.

Claiming additional hours – Each customer must sign the timesheet agreeing the amount of time each gardener spends on site.

4.10

Details of possible fraud	Employees	Collusion	Likelihood	Possible control
IT Theft of customer pricing due to open access to files	Accounts, IT	None	High	Authorised access only to customer pricing files, password protected
Payroll Wages payments overstated on timesheets	Production hourly paid	None	High	Supervisor to authorise timesheets
Warehouse Taking inventory for own use or selling on	Stores, Production	Third party recipients	Medium	Warehouse and stores locked and movements controlled in and out. Regular inventory record to physical counts and differences investigated

CHAPTER 5: TECHNOLOGY AND ACCOUNTING SYSTEMS

5.1 **(a)** True

(b) True

(c) True

(d) False

5.2 A cyberattack is an attempt by hackers to gain access to, damage or destroy a computer network or system. There are three common types: malware, phishing and ransomware.

Malware – viruses hidden in an attachment to an email designed to disrupt, damage or gain entry to a computer system.

Phishing – an email is sent pretending to be from a reputable company, intended to obtain valuable information, such as banking details.

Ransomware – a programme that locks the computers and will only give the user access once a fine is paid, often in cryptocurrency.

5.3

Incident		Risk
(a)	A power cut shuts down the server in the office	Loss of data
(b)	An employee opens an attachment on an email from an unknown supplier	Phishing
(c)	An employee clicked on an email, which locked their computer, and was asked for cryptocurrency to unlock it.	Ransomware
(d)	An employee emailed a statement of account for EH Martley Ltd to EH Marley Ltd	Data issued in error
(e)	An employee met a friend for a meal on the way home from work. She locked her laptop in her car to keep it safe whilst in the restaurant.	Physical loss of equipment

5.4 **Descriptive** analytics can be used to record high volumes of data and produce monthly reports, comparing actual and budgeted information.

Predictive analytics are used to forecast future sales, using current trend information.

Prescriptive analytics assess the potential or new markets and products.

5.5 (a), (b), (e) will all improve understanding for non-financial managers.

CHAPTER 6: EFFECTIVE ACCOUNTING SYSTEMS

6.1   (b)   Two*Nine-7 – This has a mixture of letters, lower and upper case, numbers and other symbols.

6.2   No, the Accounts Payable Clerk is not correct. The payables ledger control account reconciliation reconciles the list of suppliers' balances with the summary postings on the general ledger.

Errors the reconciliation will find include:

- purchase invoices debited to supplier's accounts
- sales invoices posted to the accounts payable control account

Errors the reconciliation would not find include:

- a pricing error in a purchase invoice
- a purchase invoice posted to the wrong supplier account
- VAT in a purchase invoice posted to rent instead of VAT control
- missing credit notes
- missing purchase invoices

6.3   Refer to pages 109 to 111 for examples.

6.4

Email
To: S. Addle, Managing Director, Pedal for Miles Limited
From: S. Poak, Accountant
Subject: Proposed payroll system

Further to our recent conversation regarding the increasing fees of the payroll bureau, I set out below the main areas we would need to undertake, should we decide to bring the payroll in-house.
 	
Data collection and storage
 	
• The timesheet system we currently have in place for production staff will continue to be used as the basis for the recording of hours worked. These are currently approved by the Supervisor.
 	
• Salaried staff are paid monthly, based on their contracts.
 	
• Additional payments, eg bonuses or commission, will continue to be authorised by the appropriate Director on the 'Variation forms' we currently use for the bureau.
 	
• We will need to enter into a payroll system and keep securely details of the following for each person:
 	
    – Staff number
    – Rate of pay
    – Tax code
    – National Insurance (NI) number

    – Deductions such as pension contributions, subscriptions, court orders

    – Bank details

Processing payroll

- A payroll software package will use the above data to calculate:

    – Gross pay

    – Deductions

    – Net pay

    – Gross taxable pay to date

    – Tax paid to date

- A payments list will be generated and a BACS payment file created for authorisation

- The payroll will then need to be approved by myself

- The BACS payment will require authorisation by two signatories, then sent to the bank

- The software will generate and submit RTI, as required by HMRC

- Payslips will be generated and can be either emailed or posted

Obviously, we hold most of the data needed now, which is keep securely locked, due to its confidential data.

The next step would be to investigate payroll systems and potential staff costs. Please let me know if you wish me to proceed with this.

Best wishes

S. Poak

6.5 Purchasing non-current assets (capital expenditure)

- Capital expenditure plan produced for five or more years, in detail for the next year

- Board of Directors approve capital expenditure plan

- Tendering process using approved suppliers

- Purchase order will be authorised by senior management, in line with approved budget

Managing the non-current asset register

- Assets are barcoded and securely stored

- Ownership records are stored securely

- Regular matching of non-current assets register to physical assets and vice versa, and differences investigated

- Disposals are authorised by senior management

- Regular reconciliation of non-current asset register to general ledger for cost, depreciation and carrying value

6.6   **Inventory count procedures**

Email
To: Hamilton Rorsch, Financial Controller, Summerland Inks Limited
From: Ann Winterfold, Accountant
Subject: Inventory count procedures

Dear Hamilton,

I suggest the following procedures for the upcoming inventory count.

Procedures for inventory count in stores area

- No items are received or despatched during the count – any deliveries should be stored in a separate area to avoid double counting.
- No inventory should be moved around the factory during the inventory count.
- The last goods received note and the last goods despatch note numbers are recorded.
- All counts are completed in pairs by staff, who are independent of stores and the warehouse.
- Counts are entered onto pre-numbered inventory sheets; inventory is marked as counted using a sticker.
- All inventory sheets are returned to Finance, once an area is completed.
- As each area is counted, a supervisor will walk the location to ensure items have been marked as counted.
- Damaged or obsolete inventory is identified and marked as such on the inventory count sheet.

Procedures for finance staff

- Pre-numbered inventory count sheets are issued for each location.
- Ensure all inventory count sheets are returned and stored.
- Compare physical inventory quantity to records in inventory management system and investigate any differences prior to the inventory count being finished.
- Follow though any damaged or obsolete inventory to the valuation, to ensure it is recorded accurately.

Please let me know if you need any further information.

Best wishes

Ann

6.7   **(a)**   Segregation

(b)   Physical access controls

(c)   Management controls

(d)   Authorisation and approval

(e)   Check arithmetical accuracy

(f)   Competent personnel

CHAPTER 7: EVALUATION AND REVIEW OF ACCOUNTING SYSTEMS

7.1

Deficiencies

- There is no authorisation process over hours worked recorded on timesheets.
- There does not appear to be authorisation of new starters.
- There is no independent authorisation process when an employee leaves.
- Timesheets are not checked for arithmetical accuracy.
- The cash request is only authorised by the Assistant Accountant, based on a payroll produced by the Payroll Clerk with no additional supporting information. There is no evidence of authorisation.
- The wage packets are put together by the Payroll Clerk alone.
- The cash wages are given to the Branch Manager.
- Wages are held insecurely overnight by the Branch Manager.
- Branch Managers pay out wages alone.
- There is no authorisation and review of the monthly payroll.

Causes

- Lack of formal authorisation procedure for hours worked.
- Lack of formal system for new starters.
- Lack of formal system for when an employee leaves.
- Lack of formal authorisation procedure to ensure timesheets are accurate.
- Lack of formal procedures for requesting and obtaining cash for wages.
- Lack of formal procedures for putting together wage packets.
- Lack of formal procedures for distributing cash wages.
- Lack of formal procedures to review and approve the payroll.

Impact

- Employees could be paid for hours they have not worked in error. Potential fraud – employees could add on extra hours not worked.
- Potential fraud by Branch Manager – set up of fictitious employee.
- The Branch Manager could delay sending the Leaver form and collude with the employee to keep the wages, as they will continue to be paid – possible fraud.
- Employees could be paid for hours not worked.
- The Assistant Accountant or the Payroll Clerk could fraudulently request additional cash.
- Potential fraud – wages could be stolen by Payroll Clerk and hidden as an error.
- Potential theft of wages by Branch Manager.
- Potential theft and fraud through theft of wages held at branch by collusion with third party.
- Potential for fraud or errors in payments created by the Payroll Clerk. Leavers may continue to be paid if they have not been correctly processed.

7.2

Weakness	Impact on business
The Maintenance Depot Manager can both authorise and raise an order for the purchase of a new coach.	Coaches may be ordered unnecessarily. Significant expenditure may be incurred where there is no business need. Cashflow problems could occur.
No tender process exists for purchasing coaches.	Coaches may not be competitively priced and the business may incur unnecessary additional cost. Purchases may not be supporting sustainable practices, such as low emission vehicles.
No Board level authorisation of capital expenditure.	The business may be buying assets unnecessarily. Cashflow problems could occur.
The discount is fixed at 5% of list price as the supplier is a friend of the Managing Director.	The business may not be achieving the best possible price for capital items and be overpaying for them.
Proof of delivery is given prior to goods being inspected and passed as fit for use.	Coaches may be received and paid for, when they cannot be used by the business.
Only one person authorised the BACS payment.	Possible fraud or error for the payment. Money could be paid unnecessarily.
Maintenance Depot Manager ordered and authorises payment for coaches (by sending the signed GRN).	Potential fraud through collusion with supplier to inflate price and take the difference.
The depreciation on the spreadsheet (non-current asset register) for coaches is not reviewed periodically.	Depreciation calculations and rates may be incorrect, resulting in the non-current asset value in the financial statements being under- or over-stated.
Maintenance Depot Manager authorises disposal price for old coaches and informs accounts of buyer details.	Coaches could be sold at below market value. Possible fraud via collusion with purchaser of coach.
No reconciliation of physical coaches to asset register spreadsheet, using serial numbers.	Potential error as disposed coaches could be included incorrectly in the non-current assets register.

7.3   (a)

Strengths	Benefits to the business
Internet site linked to inventory and sales ordering module.	Existing customers can easily place orders online for items that are in inventory. The system will automatically check they are within credit limit, so the risk of an irrecoverable debt is reduced.
	The simplicity of the process makes it very quick for the customer to place orders and as the inventory is 'real time', they know the goods are produced ready to be delivered.
Promotion of products by customised email.	The customers will receive promotions in line with their previous purchasing patterns, so they are more likely to buy. The promotion is a cheap way of sending them information to entice them to purchase more items. As 70% are repeat customers, they are likely to buy.

(b)

Weaknesses	Damage to the business
The procedures for giving credit terms to new customers are inadequate, as are the credit control procedures for late payers.	By only using references to determine a credit limit, the business could be exposed unnecessarily to customers who have a poor credit history, as they are likely to send the best possible supplier references. No initial analysis of financial accounts further increases this risk.
	The credit controls procedures are not strong enough to ensure irrecoverable debts are minimised.
The procedures over the discounting of product are not sufficiently robust. The sales staff can amend the sales price on the order, prior to accepting it. There is no procedure to monitor the levels of discount being given.	The ability for staff to discount prices on the order to secure a sale could lead to the business selling products at a loss. This would reduce the profitability of the business.
	Sales staff could offer to reduce prices in return for money for the regular customers they deal with – a potential fraud. This could be a significant loss of profit, as 70% of customers are repeat customers.

7.4

Risk: Takings can be stolen from the till

Monitor

- How much do we think the shop should take compared to how it has taken
- Identified theft of takings from till

Review

- Internal audit/walkthrough to identify areas that need additional controls
- Review till discrepancy reports – recorded by till vs cash banked

Report

- Use software to highlight potential differences – till takings to cash banked
- Produce table/report showing potential differences, ie lower takings

Risk: False refunds are made to credit cards

Monitor

- How much do we think the shop should refund compared to how it has refunded
- Level of refunds made

Review

- Internal audit/walkthrough to identify areas that need additional controls
- Refunds paperwork for evidence of staff signing for false refunds

Report

- Produce table/chart that shows the level of refunds by shop to highlight shops where this may be an issue
- Use software to identify refunds by credit card, to identify any patterns
- Refunds paperwork for evidence of staff signing for false refunds

Risk: Poor system to check and record cash takings, could result in stolen takings (fraud)

Monitor

- How much do we think the shop should bank compared to how much it has banked
- Level of discrepancies - till reports to bankings

Review

- Internal audit/walkthrough to identify areas that need additional controls
- Till reports, any reconciliation paperwork and paying in slips

Report

- Produce table/chart that shows the level of discrepancies by shop to highlight shops where this may be an issue
- Use software to identify large discrepancies and compare to staff working hours
- Monthly report of till discrepancies – both unders and overs

7.5

	Political	Economic	Social	Technological	Legal	Environmental
Offer incentives for carers to purchase electric vehicles						✓
Expected wage increases due to a rise in the minimum wage					✓	
Use tracking software to record hours worked and travel time for carers				✓		
Increasing levels of customers requiring service			✓			
Low employment levels in local area making it easy to recruit staff		✓				

7.6

Political

Government policy has incentivised people to set up their own businesses. This has generated clients for Taylor, Lowbridge & Co. The current in-house accounting system used to produce accounts is proving expensive to the business, as the level of licence required for additional clients has increased.

Economic

Minimum wage regulations have led to more clients using the payroll bureau. This has led to an increase in customers. The current payroll package used is now charging per employee processed and costs to the firm are consequently higher.

Social

A trend to consider employee welfare has led to some employees being able to work from home. This has reduced productivity for the firm, so the cost per job is higher.

Clients are more confident with technology and consider they are doing most of the work previously done by the accountancy firm. It is harder for the firm to bill for reviewing information to ensure it is accurate, so client billings for this area are lower.

Technological

60% of clients are using cloud-based technology and are inputting their own data. The staff at Taylor, Lowbridge & Co. must check the accuracy of the data entry, so they must be trained in several different cloud-based systems. There will be training costs attached to this.

Legal

Tax laws are more complex, so clients need more help submitting annual tax reporting. The system used to support tax return submission is inefficient, so staff will take longer to use it. It may no longer be fit for purpose.

Environmental

Apprentices are being trained by the firm to provide accountancy services, benefitting the local community.

Employees are being allowed to work from home, reducing the impact on the environment of commuting.

CHAPTER 8: RECOMMENDATIONS AND MAKING CHANGES

8.1 As the business has experienced rapid growth, the accounting system should be **reviewed** to ensure the reporting information it provides **is fit for purpose.**

When new staff are inducted, they should be trained **in the importance of internal controls.**

A new bespoke system **would not** be a cost-effective way of improving the current system.

8.2 **Strength**

Hotels and flights are paid for by Travel America Limited after the customer has either paid the deposit or the final balance on the booking. The business will not make payments to suppliers unnecessarily.

As dollars are purchased for the year at an exchange rate fixed in advance, the business will be unaffected by changes in exchange rates when they pay for the hotels, trips and other expenses in dollars.

Weakness

The airline payments system does not go back and update the costs within the individual booking. There is no reconciliation between the cost of sales flight figure and the final amounts paid.

Potentially, where costs are incorrect in the Reservations system, they could be undercharging the customer and losing profit. Where differences occur between payment and cost, reconciliation should be made and differences investigated, as airlines could be charging the wrong fares to Travel America.

Opportunity

The review by the Manager of the booking could be used to review whether any additional sales could be made to the customer.

As they are likely to know the products very well, they could see if there is any opportunity for selling more expensive or additional tours.

Threat

The customers want to experience unique and exciting experiences. Travel America Limited needs to work closely with suppliers to ensure the customers have the best experiences possible. If the customers do not have good service, they may choose to book with other agents or decide to book independently.

The business must be protected and continue to identify innovative and unique experiences to offer to customers. The market could be researched and current and potential customers consulted to see what they want.

NB. For weaknesses, you could also have there are no supplier payment reconciliations being undertaken for hotels. Hotel costs could be incorrectly stated or missed.

8.3   *Internet site*

The internet site could be improved to interact with inventory, not simply be an online catalogue.

This would reduce the need for Sales to confirm order details and prices and so save time. It would also improve the customer service.

Sales discounts

Sales discounts should be authorised by a senior member of staff eg the Sales Director.

This would avoid the possibility of sales staff colluding with customers to give them large discounts and receive part of the savings. Sales discounts would be minimised, maintaining the profitability of the business.

Payments by 'one-off' customers

There should be a clear procedure to identify 'one-off' customers who pay by bank transfer or PayPal have paid for the goods prior to them being despatched. The order should be marked as 'cash paid'. It should only be sent to the Warehouse once this has been done. All orders for credit customers should clearly state they are a credit customer on the order.

This will avoid any accidental despatch of goods prior to payment being received. This will limit the likelihood of an irrecoverable debt in the business.

Match despatch note to order and physical goods prior to despatch

The despatch note should be matched to the order and the goods compared to both prior to being sent out to the customer. The Warehouse staff should sign this as evidence of the review.

This will avoid despatching the wrong goods to a customer, as the goods could be costly to get back.

Signed proof of delivery with order

Signed proof of delivery should be kept with the order in the accounts department.

Customer queries can be easily resolved by referring to the signed despatch note.

8.4 **(a)**

Weakness	Potential problem	Recommendation
The clocking in system is open to abuse, as the manager is not present when staff clock in or clock out.	Staff could clock each other in or out, giving them extra hours worked. The staff could be paid for hours not worked.	A member of management should be present as staff clock in and clock out to ensure they are not claiming additional hours incorrectly.
Each hotel manager has the authority to advertise for and employ staff with no other authorisation.	Staff could be hired unnecessarily. Fictitious employees could be put onto the payroll and paid – potential fraud.	The Area Manager should authorise all adverts and new starters. All new staff need to sign the New Starter Form. This will remove the threat of fraud and avoid staff being employed unnecessarily.
Each hotel manager is able to complete all the paperwork for a new starter.	A new starter could be fictitiously added to the payroll and paid. Potential fraud.	The Area Manager should meet, ID and authorise new staff.
The hotel employs many casual staff on zero-hours contracts, who are from out of the area. There is a high staff turnover.	The staff may not be motivated to provide good customer service. They may be unable to earn enough to live comfortably.	The hotel should review staffing levels and consider offering contracts for people in the local area for 35 hours per week on a three month basis to cover the summer period. The customer service would be improved and overtime would be minimised. This would support sustainable practices.
The clocking in system is not linked to the payroll system. Hours and overtime are entered manually by the Payroll Clerk.	Errors could occur in the input of hours and overtime. The process is very inefficient.	Integrate the clocking in system to the Payroll system. The Payroll Clerk can undertake other duties with the time saved. Errors will not occur in the hours recorded for payment.
The BACS payment is authorised by the Financial Controller, using just the BACS payment list.	The Payroll Clerk could enter staff on the payroll fictitiously and commit fraud. Potential fraud risk.	Two people, including a Director, should authorise the BACS payment, with the payroll reports as supporting documentation.

(b) Cost-benefit analysis

Savings:

Payroll Clerk's time 3 hrs x £15	£45.00 per week
Employer costs (NIC, pension 15%)	£6.75 per week
Total saving	£51.75 per week

Total saving per year	£2,691.00

Costs

Software costs	£500.00
Net saving	**£2,191 per year**

Other non-quantifiable factors

– Risk of hours being incorrectly paid reduced

– More motivated Payroll Clerk

– Ability of the Payroll Clerk to support the Accounts Team

– Payroll Clerk may resent change in role

(c) Problem

The clocking in system hours could be incorrectly loaded into the payroll system. The company could pay staff for hours or overtime they have not worked.

The Payroll Clerk may not be adequately trained to ensure the data transfer happens properly.

Controls to put in place

The Payroll Clerk will need to be trained in the new procedures.

The software should be tested for a period of time using test staff data, to ensure it is working correctly.

When the system goes 'live' the Financial Controller and the Payroll Clerk will need to reconcile all the data line by line, to ensure it has been transferred over correctly, including the basic and overtime split. This process should be repeated for at least four weeks, in case any anomalies occur.

The Financial Controller should set up exception reports to identify where employees are paid significantly more or less than the previous payroll and investigate them.

8.5

Characteristic	Associated	Not associated
Decreases risk of loss of data	✓	
Speeds up the implementation process		✓
Low cost		✓
Increased workload on staff temporarily	✓	

8.6

Suggested change	Social	Corporate	Environmental
Install new motion sensitive lighting			✓
Purchase inventory using 12 months supply contracts, to secure beneficial discounts		✓	
Sponsor local high-achieving employees through local pottery design course	✓		
Invest in new inventory management system to reduce inventory holding levels and warehouse requirements		✓	

8.7

(a)

Costs	£
Staff training costs (3 staff x 2 days x £400)	2,400
Cost of linking system	15,000
Yearly fee – Design & Surface Ltd	5,000
Hardware costs	4,500
Benefits	
Additional sales (£180,000 x 40%)	72,000
(Net cost)/benefit	45,100

(b) **Any four from:**

- Will existing staff be able to use the new system to order/price the custom tables correctly?

- Initially sales ordering will be slower – lower productivity due to learning curve effect

- How will the new system be implemented – controls over transition?

- What will the impact be on production times for using new materials?

- Reliance on Design & Surface Ltd for supply of materials by Footy for Fun Ltd – is this a concern?

(c)
- Investment in new system should be made

- Financial benefit initially is £45,100

- Higher sales likely – cost-benefit analysis only based on one customer

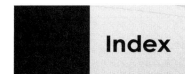

Index

for your notes

for your notes

for your notes